SITUATION AND SELF

David K. Reynolds, Ph.D.

The moon outside my window
Is usually the same moon,
But as soon as there are plum flowers
It becomes a different moon.

In the bottomless bamboo basket
I put the white moon;
In the bowl of mindlessness
I store the pure breeze.

--Miura and Sasaki, 1965

TABLE OF CONTENTS

Introduction

I consider myself a rather ordinary fellow who has had some extraordinary experiences. For example, the National Institute of Mental Health funded a study in which I became a researcher/patient in order to see what life is like for suicidal people in a mental hospital; I've lived in Buddhist temples and practiced Buddhist based psychotherapies in Japan and in the United States; I taught in a well known medical school although I'm not a physician, and listened to the stories of dying folks in nursing homes and death wards. It has been an interesting life.

Over the past fifty years my research has taken me to natural disaster sites and mental health facilities, to Japan every year, and into the homes of hundreds of victims, survivors, patients, and other ordinary and extraordinary people. The results of this research have come out in more than thirty books translated into a number of languages and a hundred articles in journals of various disciplines. Yet the research is all of a piece. Furthermore, the research fits together with my practice of what some would call psychotherapy. This book is about how what appears to be diversity actually fits together. It is about the situations in which we find ourselves and the ways in which we interpret those situations.

The contents of the book you are reading are dead center relevant to some main issues faced by anthropologists and psychologists over the past fifty years. While the anthropologist Maquet was criticizing Carlos Castaneda for failing to provide methodological means by which others could replicate Castaneda's inner discoveries as a Yaqui shaman, Norman Farberow and I were writing two books which used phenomenological data in the study of suicide within psychiatric settings and, moreover, provided a method by which the insights could be and were replicated and checked against other data. While anthropologists were expanding their field of interest to urban ethnic groups and weighing the values of objective, quantifiable data to supplement information from participant observation, Richard Kalish and I were finishing up a study using a carefully considered combination of participant observation, content analysis, and quota sampled interviews of Los Angeles ethnic groups. While Castaneda was writing imaginatively about being a sorceror's apprentice I was making annual trips to Japan to become a Morita therapist. While anthropologists and psychiatrists wrote about the theoretical impossibility of practicing non-Western psychotherapies in Western cultural contexts I was testing Morita therapy and Naikan therapy in Los Angeles and finding them understandable and helpful to Western clients.

Although my doctorate is in anthropology my work is relatively unknown to anthropologists; much of it is published in journals of psychology and psychiatry. Some of it is in the relatively inaccessible Japanese language. The methodological and theoretical content has been spread thinly, scattered here and there in specialty publications.   In this book I have pulled together what I have thought and done over the past forty years or so.   The contribution, if one there be, may be judged from this overview and from the more detailed publications to which this consolidation refers. Whatever its worth to others, my academic life is set out here for all to see.

The theme that threads through these pages is the notion of the situated self. From George H. Mead and the symbolic interactionists who argue that the self is socially constructed, from the Buddhist psychologists who argue that the self is a social fiction, and from the phenomenological perspective of experiential research we are led to an understanding of the situationally-determined, ever-changing self. A further step takes us to situated explanations of human behavior.

What is offered here is not theory alone, but a beginning methodology for utilizing the theory and verifying hypotheses derived from it. It is a small step toward incorporating phenomenological data into the realm of science.

Suicide and Symbolic Interaction

"By my fourth hospital day the depression had begun to lift; people seemed to care about my staying alive; I began to hope. We were taken to a recreation area in the afternoon. I was free to mingle with patients from several wards. The sun was warm, the grass inviting, the faded lawn chairs...But where was the aide who was supposed to be watching me? He, like the others, was off playing basketball. He didn't care that I was on Suicide Observation Status. His game was more important than my life. It dawned on me that the staff had been making a fool of me. How simpleminded I had been to believe that these strangers could ever really care about my life. I was just another increment of nuisance and work for them.

"I wandered around the area testing garden hoses for flexibility and fit as methods of hanging myself. No one paid any attention to the small fellow in baggy hospital blues. The others were all engrossed in their worlds, and I really didn't exist for them then. The hoses weren't going to suit my purpose, I had decided. Then, as I headed for a chair, I stumbled on a worn length of weathered rope lying in the grass.

"Joy! and Fear! and the beginnings of a consuming anger that could emerge now that a mode of expressing it had been found. I would show them! I sat in the chair in plain sight of my fellow patients and tied a hangman's knot in the rope. No one asked what I was doing, no one tried to restrain me, no one told an aide, no one seemed to notice at all. My stomach felt empty, hollow, and hot. I couldn't share my anger at the uncaring staff even with my patient peers now because they were indifferent to my death, too.

"It was all decided now. No other alternative presented itself nor did I seek one. The only out, the only way I could punish them and avenge myself and disturb their holy routine and show them I meant business and escape any punishment they might wish to visit on me and mock and hate and spit on them all--the only way-- was to hang myself.

"I carried my rope (how precious it had become, my conspirator now) to the tree hidden behind the barbecue pit. I threw the rope up over the limb..." (Reynolds and Farberow, *Suicide: Inside and Out*, 1973)

This story is mine. Norman Farberow and I set ourselves the task of studying, from the inside, why patients on psychiatric hospital wards make attempts at killing themselves. So I had to learn how to become depressed and suicidal. The means by which I learned to enter and leave the "fortress" of depression is described below. But first let me explain why we thought it to be necessary.

There are, of course, other ways to find out about suicide in mental hospitals. We began with several of them. One way is to gather statistical information about the sorts of hospitals in which suicides occur, the diagnoses of patients who kill themselves, the medications, family histories, ages, occupational histories, and the like. Another way is to interview the staff members of psychiatric hospitals, asking for their observations and impressions. Still another way is to interview the patients themselves--patients who knew others who committed suicide; patients who had attempted suicide themselves, patients who were being observed as potential suicide threats at the moment. Yet another way of exploring the problem is to observe what occurs on these psychiatric wards, to watch what life is like for suicidal patients and the staff personnel who take responsibility for protecting them from themselves. We did all of that. We tabulated and interviewed and observed. We even participated in ward life during group meetings and other therapy sessions. And we brought community research and therapy experience with suicide from the Los Angeles Suicide Prevention Center. Nevertheless, with all of this information, with all of our theoretical expertise in this research area, something vital was missing from our understanding of suicidal behavior on psychiatric hospital wards.

A suicidal act is both intensely personal and intricately social. A particular circumstance may appear to provoke the suicide, but the way the patient perceives the circumstance is as important as the situation itself. To miss the contribution of the self in actively constructing the interpretation of what is happening is to ignore a critical factor in the dynamic interplay of events leading to life and death decisions.

Blumer (1962) is a sharp critic of traditional psychological, anthropological, and sociological studies that ignore the individual's construction of reality:

"Sociological thought rarely recognizes or treats human societies as composed of individuals who have selves. Instead, they assume human beings to be merely organisms with some kind of organization, responding to forces which play upon them. Generally, although not exclusively, these forces are lodged in the make-up of the society, as in the case of 'social system,' 'social structure,' 'culture,' 'status position,' 'social role,' 'social norm,' and 'values.' The assumption is that the behavior of people as members of a society is an expression of the play on them of these kinds of factors or forces. This, of course, is the logical position which is necessarily taken when the scholar explains their behavior or phases of their behavior in terms of one or other of such social factors. The individuals who compose a human society are treated as the media through which such factors operate, and the social action of such individuals is regarded as an expression of such factors. This approach or point of view denies, or at least ignores, that human beings have selves--that they act by making indications to themselves. Incidentally, the 'self' is not brought into the picture by introducing such items as organic drives, motives, attitudes, feelings, internalized social factors, or psychological components. Such psychological factors have the same status as the social factors mentioned: they are regarded as factors which play on the individual to produce his action...

"The social behavior of people is not seen as built up by them through an interpretation of objects, situations, or the actions of others. If a place is given to 'interpretation,' the interpretation is regarded as merely an expression of other factors (such as motives) which precede the act, and accordingly disappears as a factor in its own right. Hence, the social action of people is treated as an outward flow or expression of forces playing on them rather than as acts which are built up by people through their interpretation of the situations in which they are placed." (ibid. p. 143)

In other words, according to Blumer an adequate schema for understanding suicide (or any human behavior) in psychiatric hospitals (or any setting) must incorporate a notion of the interpreting self which keeps on indicating or constructing the reality in which it operates. This theoretical position is called symbolic interaction. Symbolic interaction holds that we are constantly selecting and evaluating information from the situations in which we find ourselves. This information is used creatively to further interpret the situation and to interpret ourselves in that situation. "Self consciousness is the activity of viewing oneself from the standpoint of others...We come to know who we are through others' responses to us." From this point of view we are all constantly reinterpreting who we are and what circumstance we are in in light of our constantly changing perspective on a constantly changing environment.

Symbolic interaction theory seems to make intuitive sense. We do seem to reevaluate ourselves in the light of others' praise and criticism. As my mother grew older she became increasingly sensitive to slips of memory and incremental physical handicaps that accompany aging. She appeared to be reevaluating herself in terms of her attention to these changes and in terms of others responses to these changes and in terms of her evaluation of others' responses to her changed evaluation of herself, and so on. In a similar way the depressed person seems to be using information to validate a changing self view (what information might be used is described below), notices how others seem to be responding to his activities with this changing self view, uses others' responses to further validate his view of how helpless he is and how little they care about him, and so forth.

Criticism has been leveled at symbolic interaction because of the apparent impracticality of studying this "looking glass self" we all possess, or, more carefully, which is us. How would one go about researching the means we use to note and interpret the situations in which we operate? How would one demonstrate the usefulness of the theory in explaining human behavior? How could one develop hypotheses from the theory and check these hypotheses against concrete data? How can the scientist make operational this concept of symbolic interaction?

Again, Blumer (1962) offers a general suggestion:

"Insofar as sociologists or students of human society are concerned with the behavior of (humans), the position of symbolic interaction requires the student to catch the process of interpretation through which they construct their actions. This process is not to be caught merely by turning to conditions which are antecedent to the process...Nor can one catch the process merely by inferring its nature from the overt action which is its product. To catch the process, the student must take the role of the (human) whose behavior he is studying...the process has to be seen from the standpoint of the acting unit."

Stryker (1959) agrees, "The fundamental methodological principle of symbolic interaction: the demand that the investigator see the world from the point of view of the subject of his investigation." For the symbolic interactionist it is that very process by which we reflexively and dynamically interpret ourselves-in-our-world which is of great interest. Moreover, we cannot afford to ignore this process if we want to understand suicidal behavior. Followed to its logical conclusion it appears that the only way to study suicide in these settings is to study it from the inside--to make the researcher depressed and suicidal and enter the wards as a patient. The book, *Suicide:Inside and Out*, is an account of such a research project.

We called our research method "experiential research." It is one way of applying symbolic interaction theory to the real world. It is important to recognize what experiential research is not. First of all, it is not role playing. The suicidal persona we created for our research, David Kent, was admitted to a psychiatric ward in which staff and patients took him to be genuinely depressed and suicidal. Psychological tests, introspective reports, observations by professionals, and psychophysiological changes consistently supported the conclusion that Kent was in a state indistinguishable from genuine depression. We selected the name "David Kent" because my full name is David Kent Reynolds; it was a name easy for me to remember, and it represented a part of me. We intended to make this suicidal identity a part of me, too.

Secondly, experiential research is not participant observation. Unlike the traditional anthropological participant observer, Kent occupied a role slot already existing in the social system of the psychiatric ward, i.e., he was a patient, not an outsider observing on the ward. Clearly, in order to do this sort of research it is essential to enter a social system which admits newcomers with some minimal preparation. For example, it is relatively easy to become a mental patient, a stockroom clerk, a dishwasher. But to enter the role of surgeon, nuclear physicist, or Iranian would be more difficult for most of us. Of course, there is no restriction on conducting experiential research on the identities and roles we already occupy in everyday life.

Then what is experiential research? It involves oscillating observations of inner experience and outer environment (we shall deal with this dichotomy somewhat differently later) while occupying a situated identity in a particular social system. In one sense, experiential research approximates the key informant technique. In this case, however, the researcher and key informant are one and the same. This arrangement provides obvious advantages in terms of accessibility and communication of information. It is a method of reinserting phenomenological reporting into the domain of science.

Ions (1977) points out that the term "empirical" has come to mean the opposite of what it once meant:
"The presence of practical observation *based on experience* (not conclusions based on the statistical manipulation of aggregated data)...ought to be the distinguishing characteristic of 'empirical' social science." (p. 150, emphasis in original.) Ions recognizes that the goal of a completely objective, value free social science is impossible. He points out that quantified evidence is always evidence based on projections of our visions of reality. In other words, all science is participant observation. He argues for a human science based not on attempted detached observation and lifeless quantification but on experienced participation of the sort somewhat like that undertaken in our suicide research.

Let us look at a few issues raised by this method of operationalizing symbolic interaction theory. The first issue has to do with reliability and validity. What sorts of guarantees do we have that the information provided by the introspective accounts of the experiential researcher could be replicated by another researcher? What can be done to evaluate the honesty of the reports? What part of the findings can be attributed to the subjective perspective of the researcher and what part to the occurrence of situational pressures? Such questions are legitimate scientific queries, yet from the perspective of symbolic interaction they reflect an inadequate understanding of what is being pursued by this research strategy. Nevertheless, we made efforts to deal with these issues.

David Kent was sent into five psychiatric settings and two demonstration settings. Through these experiences we have begun to see what perceptions seem to be coming from Kent's biases and what elements seem to be coming from the environment. In the next chapter I shall describe a project in which Kent and a second experiential researcher were sent into the same setting at the same time.

Comparative data help us calibrate our researcher-instrument. In all of our experiential research we conduct debriefing sessions with other role members in the setting following the live- in phase. Their complementary perspectives on Kent's existence in the setting offer important alternative interpretations of events and people.

There is a built in bias, of course. Kent identifies with his fellow patients. He is committed to the improvement of their lot as he sees it. That bias is a mixed blessing. At least the bias is clear and specified. And, considering our research purpose-- creating settings in which fewer mental patients will want to commit suicide--the bias in perspective is precisely what we want.

Let's consider the ethics of such research for a moment. In our research we obtained permission from the staff to conduct experiential research in their facility. They didn't know who would be living in nor did they know when the person would arrive. The contract was to exchange ordinary treatment for feedback on how to improve life for patients after the live-in study was concluded. Fortunately, a number of institutions volunteered so that we were able to select from among them. We chose research sites on the basis of sizes, location, ethnic composition, and so forth with an eye to broad variability. After Kent was discharged, his other self was revealed to staff. They made the decision whether to tell Kent's fellow patients of the research. In four of the five psychiatric settings the staff invited us to explain our research to patients, as well. Our experience has been (and this point is supported by other researchers' accounts in the literature of live-in studies--see Reynolds and Farberow, 1976) that the great majority of patients are pleased to have someone share their world and tell of ward life from a patient's perspective. I was still welcomed by staff and patients in all five settings after the research.

I will not suggest general guidelines or limits to research based on ethics. I believe that each study should be evaluated on the basis of the study's purpose and methods, the participating investigators, the needs of the people in the research setting, the potential use and abuse of the collected data, and the merits of alternative methods.

The advantages of experiential research are characteristic. An inside perspective of a social system is generated. The data are immediate and concrete, allowing for fruitful hypothesis generation and practical suggestions for implementing beneficial changes with the settings. The impact of the social system on the individual is studied directly at the nexus of that impact. There is personal reward for the researcher, too. Adopting another identity broadens one's life, extends one's empathic capacity, and offers the humbling insight that any identity any time is a fragile lattice supported by our immediate social world. The experiential researcher finds himself/herself literally becoming another person.

Let us turn now to the project itself. Having obtained a grant from the National Institute of Mental Health to conduct such research it became necessary to create a believable, realistic depressed experiential researcher for admission to the local Veterans Administration hospital. The ward was selected and permission obtained from staff for the research to take place at some unstated time. The creation of David Kent was about to begin.

A history for David Kent was developed by the staff at the Los Angeles Suicide Prevention Center. The history included characteristic elements of high risk suicidal individuals such as a previous history of suicide attempts. Efforts were made to exaggerate aspects of the researcher's recalled history and incorporate them into Kent's life story. The more similar the two, the easier the identification and the easier recollection of the history. Videotaped practice sessions took place with professionals taking personal history information from the researcher. Reynolds learned to take on the slumped posture of Kent, the shallow breathing with occasional sighs, the slowed responses and passive resistance. In the behavior were the seeds of genuine feeling. In the doing of Kent came the feeling of Kent. Using a cognitive approach (Beck, 1967) at the same time Reynolds repeated again and again to himself "It's hopeless." "I'm helpless." "Nobody can do anything for me." "Life isn't worth living."

I have acting experience, playing the male lead role in a television program in Los Angeles. With practice I found that I could ride slight slopes in my ordinary mood cycles down into depression (and out again when the research was completed.) After the psychiatric hospital ward study was completed merely returning to the dayroom on the ward where Kent had lived helped stimulate depressed feelings necessary for subsequent projects.

Symbolic interaction provides an answer to questions I am frequently asked in relation to this study. "Were you really David Kent? Or were you just acting or role playing?" "You knew all along that you were doing research, didn't you?" My reply is that there times when I was only David Kent. But that is not so unusual. We all have multiple identities; we are all different people in different settings. An entire chapter below is devoted to this topic. The point here is that when our social world, such as the psychiatric ward on which Kent lived, mirrors back toward us a particular image it is very difficult not to become the person in the reflection. As Stryker (1959) put it,

"Others validate identities by behaving in appropriate ways, ways in which further performance in terms of the identity is possible. If these cues are not provided, then such performance is no longer possible, and the identity will fade." (p. 381)

And thus we see how it is that Kent can return to the Reynolds identity. Part of the emergence from depression involves returning to social settings in which a healthier image is reflected back by my surrounding others. Other tactics include increased physical activity and stimulus input (even though Kent doesn't feel like making such effort), engaging in meaningful and pleasurable behaviors, and avoidance of the physical setting, clothing, and so forth which are reminders and stimuli for the Kent identity.

The chronicle of Kent's observations and experiences during his two-week stay on locked and open wards is to be found in the book, *Suicide: Inside and Out*. Here I want to give an account of some of the aspects of the depressed interpreting self that we discovered with this study. Depression is a fortress, a way of withdrawing and defending one's self from life. It involves no self-extending risk, no gambling to achieve success. Failure is assumed from the start. Success is seen as a setup for even greater failure in the future. The depressed person seeks social validation of the low self-esteem. I've been right all along, Kent thought with bitter satisfaction, no one genuinely cares about me. Every slight is noted, every hinted criticism, every signal that the other is tired of giving. Emotions and attitudes of others filter through the layers of depression, although cognition and memory functions are disrupted. The depressed person tends to have a narrowed visual field, often tunneled down toward the floor. The approach to problem solving is generally narrowed, too. Kent tended to see only single solutions to problems, and those were often impossible to achieve.

The information offered above suggests something about the self who was doing the interpreting of events. In this work I am equally interested in situations as determinants of behavior. What sorts of situations prompted suicidal thought and behavior on these wards? Often they were circumstances in which the depressed person's self concept was undermined by communications from others emphasizing his impotence, unimportance, and empty future. In a sense, these communications were social validations of and elaborations on themes that were already part of the patient's conceptual baggage as described above (and learned, presumably, in earlier settings from significant others). In the psychiatric hospital the powerlessness of patients is clear and pervasive (Deane, 1961; Weitz, 1972). The patient's life must conform to a schedule that is designed for the convenience of the staff. To give an example, a televised all-star basketball game was suddenly interrupted midway through so that all of the patients on Kent's ward could be marched over to the scheduled recreation for the evening, a movie.

Partly in response to these situational pressures patients withdrew, became disorderly and confused, formed coalitions for exchange of scarce goods and mutual protection, subverted staff goals, destroyed property, displayed violent outbursts, escaped, and entertained self doubts that contributed to suicidal activity.

In the next chapter we look at the situational pressures which face the psychiatric patient following discharge from the hospital. Again the method of research is the "risky" experiential method. Yet, as Blumer (1962) has remarked,
"To try to catch the interpretative process by remaining aloof as a so-called 'objective' observer and refusing to take the role of the acting unit is to risk the worst kind of subjectivism--the objective observer is likely to fill in the process of interpretation with his own surmises in place of catching the process as it occurs in the experience of the acting unit which uses it." (p. 146)

Aftercare and Experiential Research

"In defending a social theory of mind we are defending a functional, as opposed to any form of substantive or tentative, view as to its nature. And in particular, we are opposing all intracranial or intra-epidermal views as to its character and locus. For it follows from our social theory of mind that the field of mind must be co-extensive with, and include all the components of, the field of the social process or experience and behavior: i.e., the matrix of social relations and interactions among individuals, which is presupposed by it, and out of which it arises or comes into being. If mind is socially constituted, then the field or locus of any given individual mind must extend as far as the social activity or apparatus of social relations which constitutes it extends; and hence that field cannot be bounded by the skin of the individual organism to which it belongs." (Mead, 1934, p. 223, footnote)

Fifty years ago more suicides occured among psychiatric patients during trial visits and leaves outside the hospitals than within them. Intriguing, is it not? Just at the time that the patient's mind was considered sufficiently improved to permit trips outside the hospital, suicide became the greatest danger. Could it be that the mind, "socially constituted," finds itself in matrices of social relations outside the hospital setting which provoke its self destruction? This question prompted the following research project. We selected a number of psychiatric aftercare facilities in the Los Angeles area and sent our experiential researcher into four of them. In the process we refined our research methods while "calibrating" our researcher instrument. The detailed account of this research may be found in the second book of the suicide trilogy, *Endangered Hope:Experiences in Psychiatric Aftercare Facilities.*

David Kent was "placed" (the term suggests a passive, pawn-like quality) by his social worker in a succession of four aftercare facilities ranging in size from a Family Care Unit housing three residents to a Board and Care Home with over one hundred residents. These research sites were selected from a number of facilities that had invited us in writing to conduct research at their locations. As before, the researcher's identity would not be disclosed to staff until the debriefing meeting following the live-in phase. Kent lived in these facilities for periods up to a month.

Quality of life in these facilities is suggested by the following excerpts from Kent's journal:

"Time is structured differently here than in the 'normal' world. There are a few fixed anchor points (meals, the facility's bus schedule, the times the canteen opens and closes, etc.), but there is a great deal of drifting unspoken-for time in between. Jerry B. tries desperately to fill it in with games and sleep. Many residents use conversation to fill it. Some pace, others hallucinate. One guy uses the TV (almost 'owns' the TV, it's so important to him all day). But many of us, to some degree or another, have learned to relax and simply note the passage of time--doing nothing. It's an art that takes practice like any art. If nothing else, it extends life--perhaps not objectively but subjectively...

"I found my paperback science fiction book laying on a table in the patio as I passed through. It reminded me of all the things I've been forgetting lately--my sweater (perhaps it's on the bus or at my VA detail assignment), books, my swim trunks in the bathroom, and so forth. It's as if my mind is elsewhere. David Kent is particularly bothered by these lapses. Staying at this Board and Care Home is safe and easy, but it's a step toward easy withdrawal, too. So I feel forced to go even before I'm ready because perhaps I'll be even less ready later...

"As I withdraw a bit this morning, lying in bed, the sounds of activity outside my room mock me and emphasize the difference between me and others and the uncaring quality of others who can go on with their lives while I am sad, not even wondering why I'm not among them. Such is the selfishness of the depressed." (Reynolds and Farberow, 1973, pp. 265-266)

In moving from the psychiatric hospital ward into an aftercare facility Kent felt anxious and sad. He was being forced to leave the small society of his ward and go out into a different, unknown social world. The ward had been a dull and restricted environment, but it had become familiar, the interactions were choreographed predictably. His movement toward discharge meant success to the staff. Now he must go out alone and face the task of creating a new identity in an unfamiliar setting.

We begin to see how it is the self interpreting a situation which determines behavior. The professional staff at the hospital who perceived Kent's improvement lauded his discharge (though many believed it was too soon yet). Kent interpreted leaving to be a threat. I am reminded of similar situations in which my interpretation of reality was not that of another person's. For example, while conducting research on a long-term medical care ward in a general hospital I encountered an elderly man in a wheelchair. He wore old dirty no-longer-white gloves as he wheeled himself around from place to place. In other respects he seemed reasonably neat and clean. I suggested to him that he wash his gloves now and then. He patiently informed me that in the condition they were in he could leave the gloves with his wheelchair outside the canteen or in the hallway and no one would take them. To wash them would invite theft. In another case, carrying valuables around as "bag ladies" and "pack rats" do is quite a reasonable solution to lack of secure safekeeping facilities. The determination of what is valuable is definitely individualistic.

Kent's stay in these facilities provided evidence indicating that there are phases in the "career" of the ex-psychiatric patient. In these aftercare facilities he enters as a newcomer. Newcomers are allowed certain privileges. They may break some rules because they aren't familiar with them yet. They may ask questions and so forth. During their period as newcomers they are noticed and greeted, perhaps taken under the wing of an experienced resident. Between newcomer and membership status is an interim period during which the resident is neither privileged nor knowledgeable. Kent found himself most depressed and suicidal during this interim period. His self was amorphous. He was neither this nor that, not yet a fully functioning member of the small community of residents. His identity was in transition.

Ideally, there is another transition possible as the resident moves out into the larger community toward independent living. In fact, few residents do so. Most aftercare facilities are not stepping stones but warehouses for society's rejected people. In these cul-de-sacs the rewards of life are few but so are the demands. Freedom is mostly unrestricted. It is a sheltered world in which one need not compete or struggle. One need not be alone. Those who go out and succeed don't come back to tell of their success. Those who go out and fail return to talk of the difficulties of life on the outside. It is no wonder that many residents feel unready and unwilling to try life outside these limited and limiting settings.

Thus, our research strategy was to put the researcher in a situated identity in a variety of settings and allow him to report on his experienced reality. To talk about his depression without providing information about the setting would be meaningless. Psychological data without being situated is meaningless. Similarly, it is insufficient to describe the setting from some outside perspective without providing information about the psychological and social state of the observer. Clearly, different role groups in these facilities saw their environments differently. We could get at some of these differences during the debriefing sessions with staff and with residents following the experiential research. The literature provided further perspectives on these life settings. Furthermore, within role groups there were individual differences in perceptions of the settings. For example, some staff members seemed to be emphasizing all cues that pointed to their being different from residents in their care. Others seemed to notice and dwell on the similarities between themselves and their charges. Even in the case of individuals the perception of the setting changed from day to day. The aftercare facility looked rather different when one was having a "bad day", for example. There was no standard perception of the facility, no unchanging viewpoint or self from which to perceive it, no unchanging facility to perceive.

The reasonable course to allow some objectivity into this study of flux was to obtain comparative information from various standpoints. As noted we could interview residents and staff, and we were able to examine the relevant literature. We decided to send a second experiential researcher into the largest facility at the same time Kent was there in order to begin to try to tease out what parts of Kent's observations were being strongly conditioned by Kent's psychological state and what parts were being strongly conditioned by the setting itself. Helen Sonier-Sullivan, a clinical psychologist, took on the identity of Helen Summers and was placed in a Board and Care facility at the same time as Kent.

This refinement in the method of experiential research resulted in confirmation of the important influence of the setting on the residents' behavior. Helen wrote:
"I was sitting outside with a bunch of people before lunch and there was a lot of kidding, directed especially at Larry and Joe, for sleeping so late. But as Joe put it-- what else is there to do?
"One of the things that strikes me about this particular system is the relative unproductiveness of so many of the members. I think that after a while non-productivity tends to lower the activity level and motivation and thus begins a self-perpetuating cycle. I notice that even in myself, my motivation to do anything is severely reduced and it's all I can do to establish little routines so as to keep myself moving." (Reynolds and Farberow, 1973, p. 265)

Again, accounts of experiences within the same facility by two experiential researchers were compared with accounts from other residents living there and staff perspectives obtained during post live-in debriefings. The dramatic and personal nature of experiential research facilitated interest and cooperation in making practical changes in the environments of these facilities. Suggestions for change were made at each research site, at a general meeting for aftercare facility operators in the Los Angeles area, and at various training meetings for social workers. Publications in the trade newsletter and in professional journals offered similar recommendations for change.

Specific recommendations included organizing staff and residents into small mutual responsibility groups. Newcomers could be immediately assigned to a group, and a particular member of the group could take responsibility for introducing the newcomer to the facility. Aftercare facilities need to be separated according to function with some oriented toward custodial care and some oriented toward preparing the residents for return to community life. Those facilities specializing in preparations for community living should be rewarded for each resident who leaves and lives in the community for more than six months. The system as it exists today rewards operators for keeping long term, highly medicated residents in crowded living conditions. The experiential researchers noted that the residences priding themselves in rehabilitation brought in experts to their facilities for training the residents. The residents were taught about outside living without the necessity of ever leaving their residence. Such a method defeats its own purpose. To be preferred would be satellite training facilities where commuting residents from a number of residences could learn independent living skills. Such training facilities would bring these former psychiatric patients outside of their residences onto public transportation, thus more closely approximating the sort of job situation they hope for in the future.

Our work in board and care homes and family care units confirmed many of the earlier observations about the situated nature of much "craziness." Much of what appeared at first to be odd behavior turned out to be quite functional when one understood the circumstances in which it occurred. The impotence of these rejects of society was perpetuated, though in lesser degree, in their aftercare living situations. Most of the residents themselves shared the larger society's stigma concerning the psychiatrically disturbed. Along with the "free ride" philosophy inevitably came recognition that the residents were not contributing members of society with, usually, a loss of self-esteem. Drugs, sleep, television, and other diversions kept the meaninglessness of this existence submerged for long periods, but awareness of the subtle menace within this sheltered environment surfaced from time to time.

Halfway houses and other forms of aftercare facilities are not the only settings to which psychiatric patients are discharged. Many return to their families. Our research took us next to an intensive look at a family as it accepted one of its members back from his stay in a psychiatric hospital. That study is described in the next chapter.

A Shadow in the Family

"If one approaches a distant object, he approaches it with reference to what he is going to do when he arrives there. If one is approaching a hammer, he is muscularly all ready to seize the handle of the hammer. The later stages of the act are present in the early stages--not simply in the sense that they are ready to go off, but in the sense that they serve to control the process itself. They determine how we are going to approach the object, and the steps in our early manipulation of it." (Mead, 1934, p.11)

"Mead did not question that nature--or the extra-human world--is objectively there regardless of our experience of it. He was a pragmatist, not an idealist, in philosophy. He consequently held, however, that all objects are defined as such in and through human experience. Objective nature thereby comes to possess certain characteristics by virtue of its relationship to human experiencing or mind which it would not possess otherwise...An object is always in this sense a "construct," a resultant, the kind of response which will ensue after a certain type of activity. A blackboard, for example, is what it is for us, has certain properties associated with writing in black and white, because that is the way it responds to our activity. As a symbol, an object, it stands for certain consequences in activity...From this standpoint, an object may be defined as a 'collapsed act' the sign of what would happen if the act were carried to completion...An object, thus becomes a meaningful reality to a human being because of his ability to make indications, either imaginatively to himself, or directly to others. All objects, all symbols with semantic reference, represent telescoped acts." (Troyer, 1946)

Symbolic interaction theory holds that objects take on meaning for us in terms of our real or imagined actions on them. Moreover, our actions on objects are informed by others in our social world. It is through our interactions with others (again, real or imagined) that we learn what is an object and how to act upon it. In this chapter we shall consider the socially-constructed meaning of objects and acts in the life of a suicidal and schizophrenic young man, Chuck Smith.

As indicated above, suicides among treated psychiatric patients occurred more frequently outside the hospital than within it. Our research led us to settings into which patients are discharged. Many return to their families. We decided to try to get an inside, in-depth view of the family life of at least one such ex-patient. Of course, it would be impossible to conduct experiential research within a family in the same way we were able to conduct it within the anonymity of a psychiatric hospital ward and four aftercare facilities. We did, however, find a courageous family that was willing to take in a "shadow," i.e., a researcher who would follow the discharged patient during all of his waking hours for an extended period following his release from the psychiatric hospital.

At the time of our study Chuck Smith (a pseudonym) was thirty-one years old. He had a history of at least three suicide attempts--one with sleeping pills, one with gas, and another with a gunshot wound to the chest. There were other attempts, he confided the time and means, but they are not recorded here. He complained of auditory and visual hallucinations, depression and anxiety. He was preoccupied with self-destructive thoughts. Over the years of psychiatric hospitalizations and outpatient care Chuck had developed expertise in the effects of combinations of medications on his psyche. Like many chronically disturbed persons he had developed a familiarity with psychiatric theory and a sprinkling of jargon which he didn't always use appropriately.

Chuck was a fairly intelligent young man with a good school record until military service. He had worked as a disc jockey in a small town, a taxi driver, a short order cook, and an aide in a convalescent home. He read widely and had a broad vocabulary.

When Chuck returned from the hospital again and again he was fortunate to have a family willing to support him. At the time of our fieldwork he was discharged to live with his father and mother in a one bedroom apartment. His sister lived nearby, and a married brother resided in the same city but further away. For our purposes we shall focus here on the meanings, the social constructs, which developed between Chuck and his mother, we shall call her "Jewel".

Jewel Smith was clearly the dominant figure in Chuck's life. In fact, each member of the Smith family found it necessary to develop some means of coping with Jewel's strong need to control them. She recognized her need to dominate; she, too, was a bright and insightful person. Nevertheless, she was the apparent force that maneuvered the others and held them all together at the same time.

An example of their interaction is taken from *The_Family_Shadow*: Friday Morning. 8:00. Chuck was still asleep. Jewel wanted him to go scuba diving with his sister on Sunday. "It would do him a world of good," she said. "It's the kind of group I want him to go out with: it would get rid of some of his insecurity." Dawn's scuba diving friends are very close, "almost like a family."

8:10 Mrs. Smith was in the bedroom making the bed. Beds often remained unmade until noon. But today she wanted Chuck to wake up (i.e., she wanted to control his waking) so she puttered (quietly, of course, but with enough disturbance to accomplish her purpose). Finally, she called him. Chuck replied, "Dave here?" She told him that I was. Chuck did not stir. Jewel came out to the kitchen, but she returned to the bedroom to check on Chuck when he did not get up promptly. She opened the front door (unusual behavior for that early in the morning). "It cools the house," she commented. "Seems like the house smells bad this morning." (Did a bad smell symbolize interpersonal conflict for her?) She said, partly to herself, "I've got a lot to do today. I don't know where to start." She sighed, a bit peeved at Chuck for this intuitive resistance to her beginning a busy day early. She could not prepare breakfast until he got up.

8:30 Mrs. Smith talked of buying chicken from a local take-out place. She decided that the people at the stand where she bought it once just did not know how to cook. She expected that when she tried the new place nearby, it would turn out that they did not know how to cook, either. "That much grease'll kill you." Chuck had fallen asleep again.

8:50 Chuck got up and waved to his mother. "Just like a little boy," she remarked. At the table, he dropped a spoon. In the Smith family, any mistake invariably elicited a comment. Jewel jibed, "Butterfingers." "Yes," he replied meekly, still groggy. Jewel jumped in early to tell him what she wanted him to do for her today. "Do you feel like driving me?" "No," he interrupted. "Well, do it anyway...if you want to eat." The tone was joking, but the underlying threat-message was apparent.

9:00 Mrs. Smith spoke of the enjoyment involved when the family got together to make ice cream by hand. But a piece of ice got in the gear mechanism and tore up the machine. It was broken and unfixable. Again this speech pattern of (a light, positive utterance followed by a dark, negative one.) Chuck lay on the couch with a cup of coffee.

9:30 Chuck went to pick up the mail. Mrs. Smith told me, "I don't open my husband's mail unless it's the Travel Club or the Moving Company Newsletter. Not that he keeps any secrets from me--but that's not the point!" (It was her point to begin with!)

9:35 Jewel reeled off to Chuck a series of recent tragedies involving people at the nursing home she used to manage. "They seem to think that if I'd been there, these things wouldn't have happened--but they would."

9:40 Jewel sat in the armchair lost in thought.

10:00 She headed for the bedroom. "I think I'll go lie down for a few minutes. I don't feel too well this morning."

10:30 Donna (Chuck's sister) called. Chuck answered the telephone. He told her we were all sleeping. "We're not lazy: we're tired," he told her in response to her evaluation of the three of us. Jewel emerged from the bedroom to ask if Donna wanted to talk with her.

10:35 Her telephone conversation over, Jewel went downstairs to chat with the apartment manager. Chuck sat on the couch. The rounds of the bookstores he had planned to make today did not materialize.

10:45 Mrs. Smith returned feeling chilled. "People are so rude," she said. She filled us in on the manager's problems with other tenants and the owner of the building. "Boy, I wouldn't manage one of these places again to save my life...Boy, she has got her hands full..." Chuck sat stoically, listening and smoking.

10:50 Jewel jumped up to defrost the refrigerator.

11:30 Chuck did not like the book he had been reading. He remarked, "I feel ambivalent this morning." "Well, get with it," Jewel prompted. "Get up and do something!" He retreated into the bedroom to select another book.

11:55 A Spanish-speaking Avon salesgirl, barely fluent in English, came by and sold Chuck some after-shave lotion. He was gentle and helpful to the amateurish and awkward young lady who soon returned to her baby crying in a stroller downstairs. Mrs. Smith stayed unnoticed in the kitchen and bedroom. (Reynolds and Farberow, 1981, pp. 48-50)

"After breakfast you can start putting the laundry in the car."

"You didn't empty your ashtray."

"Aren't you beginning to get a little cool, David?" I shut the door.

"Move over."

"Aren't you going to study today?"

Jewel controlled the time of the family meals, the amount eaten, the selection of foods. She picked television channels, adjusted the picture on the screen, advised where to sit while viewing. She tried to determine when Chuck drove, where, the route to take, and his driving style. Furthermore, she resisted others' attempts to control her life even to the degree of taking medication at her convenience rather than as directed.

It is within this context of control exerted on Chuck's life that we begin to see special meaning attached to Chuck's mental disorder and suicidality. What Norman Farberow and I have argued in our suicide trilogy (and others such as Liang and Braginsky and Rosenhan have argued elsewhere) is that what may appear at first to be meaningless, "crazy" behavior may become quite understandable when one considers the social context within which it is framed. Rather like the "strange and savage" customs of preliterate people come to take on rich meaning when anthropologists begin to view the world from their perspective, so the behavior of this schizophrenic, suicidal young man begins to make sense when we view it within the context of his family interaction.

As Troyer (1946) put it, "Meaning is implicit wherever there is present a certain 'triadic relation of a gesture of one individual, a response to that gesture by a second individual, and completion of the given social act initiated by the gesture of the first individual.' Meaning is, therefore, thoroughly social in origin and nature." (The internal quotation is from Mead, 1934.)

Chuck's suicide attempts take some meaning as his gesture to his mother of his ultimate independence, her response of impotence, rage, and withdrawal, and his recognition of her response. Put another way, Chuck appears to be engaged in a contest with his mother over control of his life. He has carved out a domain of behaviors over which he allows her no control. She wants him well. He will remain disturbed. She wants him alive. He will tease death. In a distorted fashion his self-destructive behavior is rooted in a healthy desire for autonomy. The tragic meaning for us is that someday Chuck may win the battle with his mother and lose his life.

Something must be written here, too, about the implications of the social construction of meaning for the research methods employed in this study. The researcher, too, finds meaning (creates understanding) through his interaction with the family members. For this investigation we decided to use an innovative research method we have called "shadowing." The aim was to so share Chuck's waking hours that a temporary identification of the shadow with Chuck would be possible. We sought to have the researcher's perspective begin to coincide or merge with that of his companion. The way to do so would be to share Chuck's social and physical world, to sleep when Chuck slept, to eat when he ate, to follow Chuck's lead through twenty four days until Chuck's readmission to the hospital.

"We recognize, of course, that distances between individuals are immense and ultimately impassable. We acknowledge, nonetheless, the capacity for intense moments of communication, as in feeling the bursting joy of another's success, in sharing overwhelming grief and sorrow at another's loss, in expressing the same words simultaneously, in 'knowing' what is going on in the mind of a relative or acquaintance, or in experiencing crowd contagion. Placed in this perspective, the process of momentary empathic identification provides a uniquely revealing insight into our subjects and increases our understanding of the behavior and the relationships of our subjects. It is within these data, derived from both the intuitive-empathic and the objective, that we hope to learn more about how suicide, schizophrenia, and family interact." (Reynolds and Farberow, 1981)

There is no doubt that the presence of an identified observer worked to bias behavior in the family somewhat. However, the shadow's presence did seem to fade into background at times, and, as all members of the family acknowledged, the researcher soon became "like one of the family." The shadow spent many nights in a sleeping bag on the living room floor of the apartment so as to be present when Chuck got up in the morning.

In passing, I might remark that shadowing taught me a great deal about myself, too. In the process of trying to be as unobtrusive as possible I learned much about the ways I make my wishes and needs known to other people in order to influence their behavior. How difficult it was to refrain from eating or mentioning my hunger when the young man had simply forgotten to eat lunch. How hard to let him make a lengthy mistake without comment or watch him spend his meager income on what I considered unnecessary or unusually high-priced items. I had to learn to follow him through doors so as not control the timing of his interactions with others. When he was in immediate danger I did consciously act to influence him--for example, when he was about to back his car into another vehicle. There are limits to this goal of being inconspicuous. Chuck's shadow became his sidekick, his confidant--not ignored, but very soon not obviously "played to" as an audience, either. One of the unanticipated responses from my body confirmed that I was beginning to share some of the meaning of Chuck's world. Whenever Jewel began saying something positive I found myself wincing, my stomach tightened. Looking back over the notes a trend that was quite obvious and consistent but had gone foolishly unnoticed became clear. Jewel's positive statements were quite often followed by negative, depressing ones:

"Rome is beautiful, but the Romans are the most cold, callous...people I've ever seen."

In the store Jewel commented on the beautiful plants on sale then she said that one of her ferns had died.

"He's one of the few Italians I like--a nice fellow, not like most of the young people these days. He's clean. His roommate was a filthy pig."

The pattern is clear. The forthcoming critical barb undermined the positive preceding statement. Interestingly, one of Chuck's primary symptoms was his perception that the world about him shifted rapidly throughout the day between bright cheerfulness and dark negativity. This abrupt oscillation was quite disturbing and showed a remarkable parallel to his mother's speech pattern.

Shadowing is a step removed from the subject-researcher identification of experiential research. Yet is does allow participation in the subject's social world with consequent access to some of the shared meanings of that world. In the suicide trilogy studies described in the previous brief chapters we learned something about suicidal behavior in various social settings, something about the social construction of meaning embedded in that and all behavior, but also something about the social construction of the self (or selves). To this fragile latticework of self we turn our attention in the next chapter.

The Breeze in the Bottom of the Bowl

"Whatever be the acting unit--an individual, a family, a school, a church, a business firm, a labor union, a legislature, and so on--any particular action is formed in the light of the situation in which it takes place...The acting unit necessarily has to identify the things which it has to take into account-- tasks, opportunities, obstacles, means, demands, discomforts, dangers, and the like; it has to assess them in some fashion and it has to make decisions on the basis of the assessment. Such interpretative behavior may take place in the individual guiding his own action, in a collectivity of individuals acting in concert, or in 'agents' acting on behalf of a group or organization. Group life consists of acting units developing acts to meet the situations in which they are placed." (Blumer, 1962, p. 145)

In an excellent and concise overview of a subset of cognitive development literature Shweder (1982) cites various studies indicating different levels of cognitive functioning for the same individual depending on the task (read "situation") presented to him/her. "The person who functions at a formal operational level on one task is not typically the same person who functions at a formal operational level on a second task...The message of these studies is that cognitive functioning is not independent of the details of the task." (pp. 357-358) A noteworthy observation--we cannot separate the functioning of the person from the situation within which the act is embedded.

Edgerton and Bercovici (1976) carried out a follow-up study of mentally retarded persons discharged into the community. They found three complications that reflected on previous research into social adjustment of this population. First, the adjustment of some persons fluctuated markedly, even when viewed from week to week. Second, previous research had looked almost exclusively at personality variables in trying to predict adjustment. Consideration of the detailed environmental settings into which the patients were released was generally lacking. Finally, the criteria for "adjustment" seem so linked to specific person and setting variables as to be either meaningless or pragmatically useless when defined in blanket, abstract ways.

Such weakness in theory and research is not limited to follow-up studies in mental retardation. Almost the entire literature based on fixed choice, non-situation-specific questions from interviews and questionnaires is equally meaningless. Take, for example, a question from my own early research (Kalish and Reynolds, 1976): "If you were dying would you want to be told? (Yes, no, don't know)" There are all sorts of things I need to know before being able to answer the question sensibly. Dying of what? Where am I at the time? Who would tell me? What certainty level do they have? Is it likely to be hours or days until death? What physical condition am I in? What else have I lost recently? In other words, I must know the circumstances in order to provide a meaningful answer to this question or any other question of this type.

Several years ago I was conducting a pilot study on elderly patients in nursing homes in Japan. The nursing assistants were filling out checklists of behavioral observations. They kept adding notes to the bottom of the checklists. The notes read, for example, "This patient has trouble walking; he puts large amounts of food into his mouth at once; he has definite preferences about food and won't come to the dining room when certain foods are served..." "About three times a year he becomes manic; his blood pressure goes up; he talks a lot, and he becomes extremely sensitive about what others around him are doing." It seemed that the nursing assistants considered it important to add more context to the checklists. It was as if they were saying to the researcher, "You can't understand what has been checked here unless you take these other data into consideration."

The use of fixed choice non-situation-specific questions is related to the theoretical concept of a fixed character molded in early childhood and continuing unchanged through adulthood. From that outmoded point of view there is no need to specify circumstantial parameters because a dependent person will respond in a dependent way whatever the circumstances, an authoritarian individual will be consistently authoritarian, an oral person will reflect orality, and so forth. Unfortunately, such consistency of character exists only in fiction and some psychological theorists' and clinicians' minds.

We sometimes speak as if each person had a single character or personality. Sometimes we notice that persons aren't behaving as we expect them to behave given our understanding of who they are. So we have various phrases like "He's not himself today," "He's in a strange mood," "What got into her?" "That doesn't sound like her at all," and so forth. Through these auxiliary ideas we try to hold on to the central concept of a single person with a single self, personality, or identity. This patching up is similar to that required years ago before the heliocentric view of the solar system was proposed.

What is needed, I think, as a first step is a view of humanity that sees us as more or less flexibly responding to the situation in which we find ourselves. I use the phrase "more or less" because it does seem that some individuals have more built in flexibility than others (although most of us are more situationally responsive than we are assumed to be). The term situation is used here to include our sociocultural world as well as our physical world. "Situation" here is what Lewin (1935) called our "life space." I use the phrase "find ourselves" to acknowledge the indisputable fact that each person perceives a situation in his/her own particular way. We perceive our situations in a unique fashion, though we are sometimes able to communicate with one another about our perceptions.

None of the above is particularly new or radical. Most psychologists and anthropologists would probably agree with the general thesis that some account must be taken of a person's situation or environment if we are to make sense of their behavior. Why is it, then, that so little research has been done on the situational responsiveness of individuals in nonexperimental settings? We have a great number of psychological experiments looking at individuals' responses to highly structured, artificial settings. We have comparative anthropological studies of group responses to natural and artificial ecological change. But we have very little observational material covering both individual behavior and natural setting in depth.

Of what use would such material be anyway? It seems to me that we pay lip service only to the idea that humans respond to situational pressures. If we genuinely accepted such a view of humankind we would have as much information about settings and their effects on individuals as we have about individuals' psychodynamics and personality structure. Once we leave the area of child studies (and even in that area the focus is almost exclusively on the parent and sibling aspects of the child's situation) we have scant data on the effects of any extra-laboratory setting on individuals. Are the settings in which adults operate too complex, too fluid, too numerous to study? I think not. Below is cited some recent research in psychology focused on the influence of situations on behavior.

The research cited in the first few chapters of this book focused on settings with strong situational pressures-- psychiatric hospitals, aftercare facilities, a family. In later chapters we shall consider Japanese psychotherapies with powerful effect because the therapists control the settings in which patients learn these lifeways. From the moment of waking to the moment of sleep the patient in these settings is reminded of "appropriate" attitudes and actions. I suspect that if we are to develop an understanding of humanity which emphasizes the responsiveness to situations it will be helpful for us to look first at those "total institutions" which exert constant and overwhelming pressure on all who enter whatever their background and personality structure.

One of the characteristic advantages of this approach is that it allows us to use the materials from anthropology, sociology, social psychology, personality psychology, political science, history, biology, and other disciplines on an equal basis. Each of these disciplines describes key aspects of situations in which humans operate and some critical tasks or concerns that are inherent in those situations. What have become sterile disciplinary boundaries vanish as the shared purpose of elucidating situational selves comes to the foreground.

One result of our efforts might be a sort of theoretical lexicon of situational structures and effects. One can envision a sort of encyclopedia such that, given a particular setting, one could assess the elements of the setting and combine the lexically meaningful effects in grammatically correct patterns to predict the sorts of situational pressures likely to be exerted. Then, taking into account one's knowledge of an individual's tendencies, one could begin to understand and predict that person's behavior in that particular setting. At this level three kinds of data are necessary to predict an individual's behavior--the effects of the elements of a setting, these effects in patterned combination, and the orientation of the person who is in the setting.

We are moving toward a much more radical situational understanding of human behavior in this chapter, but first it is necessary to prepare the reader with more evidence of the reasonableness and respectability of this milder view.

Information about a situation is necessary in order to predict human behavior. Furthermore, information about the situation or context is needed in order to interpret or find behavior meaningful. All acts are situated acts. None occurs outside of context (just as no emotion occurs outside of cognitive context). Here is a simple illustration:
1. pa
2. party
3. partying
4. He has been partying so much, he's beginning to fall apart.
5. "He has been partying so much, he's beginning to fall apart," his wife said.
6. "He has been partying so much, he's beginning to fall apart," his wife said smiling.
7. "He has been partying so much, he's beginning to fall apart," his wife said smiling to the minister.
8. "He has been partying so much, he's beginning to fall apart," his wife said smiling to the minister as they cuddled together on the parsonage couch.

9. It was winter, 1946. London lay covered in snow. "He has been partying so much, he's beginning to fall apart," his wife said smiling to the minister as they cuddled together on the parsonage couch.

With each of the above additions the meaning of the initial "pa" becomes more and more clearly defined. It only makes sense in terms of its context. It is only understandable when its surroundings are explicated. This utterance is behavior at a simple level. When we move to the level of a yes or no response to a questionnaire or a kiss between lovers the context becomes even more critical if we are to make sense of the behavior.

This element of contextual meaning affects not only the researcher or theorist who is trying to explain human action, but the actors themselves. One characteristic difficulty with simplistic attempts at situational explanations of human behavior stems from the propensity of the human mind to put meaning into situations, to interpret them. The hard line Skinnerian has trouble explaining the creative choice of words in a novel. He chooses to avoid dealing with very real phenomena such as fantasies, dreams, plans. Using a simplistic model of situational-behavioral modification I might to try to extinguish the complaining behavior of a post-operative patient by ignoring him when he complains, and by smiling and giving him attention when he is not complaining (i.e., by giving positive reinforcement for non-complaining behavior). However, once the patient realizes what I am about we have entered a whole new dimension of interaction. When he knows what I am up to he can choose to cooperate or sabotage my plans no matter how much noticing or smiling I might use to try to manipulate his behavior. The meaning he attributes to the situation will determine his response to my efforts. Any sophisticated attempt at explaining human behavior cannot afford to ignore the situational factors as interpreted by the actors. The issue of whether the situation is "out there," as part of reality or "within" the interpretive faculties of the individual or even "within" the interpretative faculties of only the researcher/analyst echoes an issue that has long plagued psychology and anthropology in various forms. Again, a radical solution to this issue will be offered later in the chapter. First a bit more needs to be said about the state of the art of situational analysis in psychology and anthropology. Magnusson (1981) edited a book with a good representation of then-current work in situational psychology. Let us examine some of its contributions and limitations.

Magnusson himself provides a scholarly and conservative overview of the field of situational psychology. Collapsing his categories somewhat there seem to be four major thrusts of research. They are: analyses of actual environments, analyses of perceived environments, classifications of individuals in terms of their responses to situations, and analyses of person-environment interactions. Magnusson clearly sees the difference between what he calls actual environment (objectively measurable) and perceived environment (requiring some sort of introspective or indirect measurement). He believes that the most sophisticated model must incorporate interactive effects between person and situation. He sees that it would be necessary to gather behavioral data across situations to tease out what are general effects of situations on all actors within them and particular characteristic responses of individuals within less powerful situations. The particular characteristic responses of individuals across situations would provide information about consistency of personality.

Within Magnusson's book are also perceptive critiques of psychology and social psychology in particular. Various suggestions for improvement of psychological science are germane, but like Howard's (1982) recommendations for psychological anthropology they skirt a possibility that opens up a whole new way of thinking about and conducting human studies. Let us see how they tread the fence of innovation but fall back on the side of tradition.

"However, it is not just the information offered directly in specific situations that constitutes the environmental influence. Indirectly, great influence is also exercised by the cognitive structures, contents, affective tones, and coping strategies characteristic of an individual's conceptions of the total world and formed in earlier confrontations with various environments. In some sense, past environments are also present." (Magnusson, 1981, p.3)

"Part of the discussion in this chapter has employed formulations about static situations as snapshots of available parts of the environment. Such analyses belong to a mechanistic person-situation interaction approach. A dynamic interaction model stresses the continuously ongoing person-situation interaction process in which individuals actively seek or avoid some situations, influence and transform situations and environments by their activities, temporarily and over time, and are influenced by situational and environmental factors at different levels of generality." (Ibid., p. 32)

"Yet theory and conceptualization do not just connect observed events; to a very considerable extent, they create the events to be explained. Thus, home runs, royal flushes epileptic seizures, homosexual panic reactions, moon shots, and black holes are events, observations, or phenomena that reflect our understanding; indeed, to varying extents, they exist and can be observed for what they are because of our understanding of them...In effect, we are informed not only by nature but by our understanding of it; what we observe is shaped by our understanding of what we see." (Bowers, 1981, p. 183)

"Nevertheless, no matter how sophisticated, well motivated, and candid the person may be, what is said by way of self- explanation is in effect a theoretical statement about the likely causes of behavior and has no special claim to the truth of the matter. Introspection simply cannot access the 'true' causal connections between action and its determinants any more than observation can discern the causal connection between external events." (Bowers, 1981, p. 193)

"When asked to predict the behavior of another person, (Western lay) observers seem to ignore information about the most typical behavior for the situation, focusing instead on the personality of the target individual...The indirect effect occurs when the perceiver explicitly focuses on the person's personality or behavior but makes an interpretation of this behavior that varies with changes in the context of observation. So, although not consciously attributing the causes of behavior to the situation, the perceiver's attributions about the other person's personality may be influenced nonetheless by aspects of the situation. For instance, if I observe some person acting cheery and friendly at a party, I may use the term extroverted as a description of their personality. However, the same behavior observed at a funeral might lead me to revise my interpretation of this person's character..." (Cantor, 1981, p. 236)

"In psychological discourse it is entirely unclear what we mean by and what we set as the boundaries of person...What we mean by situation and what we set as situational boundaries is similarly entirely unclear...For example, is my past life history a situation? Does it become objective when described by others? Is an intimate relationship, as Peterson suggests, a situation? Is the grammatical object of any sentence a situation? And finally, if the subjective environment is the person's perceptions and cognitions, the conceptual border separating person from situation fades to obscurity." (Bem, 1981, 99-100)

As Raush (1979) has pointed out when the situation becomes the perceived situation, i.e., the subjectively evaluated circumstance, it has merged with personality. The two concepts are not distinct. Arguing along similar lines we may infer from Magnusson's quote above that personality is a distillation of past situations. Furthermore, several authors (Bem among them) have argued that personality cannot exist apart from situation or be assessed apart from situation (Cantor) or be seen as a causally independent variable by either observation or introspection (Bowers). Bem concludes that the boundaries between personality and situation are eminently indistinct. Raush argues the same point from a more formal epistemological position.

Given all this recognition of the merging of the concepts of personality and situation, on close scrutiny it seems rather surprising that many of the authors in Magnusson's book on the state of the art in situational psychology proceeded to conduct research and report their findings as if they could distinguish between personality and situation. They seem to be blind to the tendency that they, like Cantor's Western lay observers, have learned to abstract the locus of causality for action in the personality. They seem to ignore the possibility that their conception of "personality" is creating the reality-for-them just as in Bower's examples of "moon shots" and "home runs". Their hypotheses about the causality of behavior are as conditioned by their situated past as is the layperson's. Bower's warning about the limits of introspection and observation apply to the psychologist as to anyone else.

What I am about to suggest here is that the most parsimonious and logical solution to this morass of confused concepts is to reduce them to one--the situation. A corollary of this recommendation is that all research becomes unashamedly experiential, even supposedly "objective" research.

It is no new idea that stability of what we call personality may lie in the continuity and stability of situations (Reynolds and Farberow, 1976). It is no recent notion that the self is created by situated events in early experience (Mead, 1934). As will be elaborated in detail in following chapters the notion that the self (or its psychologically abstracted equivalent, the personality) is a fiction has a hoary history in Buddhist psychological thought.

There are only situations. This flow of situated awareness which I call me is all that "I" will ever know about the world. One of the goals of the Buddhist based therapies described in the next chapters is to assist the student/patient to achieve an experiential sense of themselves as part of the situation or environment. The perception is rather like turning oneself inside out, becoming me-as-a-part-of-this-reality. The concept isn't so hard to play with intellectually, but to arrive at the perception takes diligent practice. One step along the way to a personal understanding of this viewpoint is to attack the notion of one me, one personality.

Again, there are only situations. To see that I am many identities, many personalities, many me's is to see that I am no identity, no personality, no me--at least I need not feel tied down to a single, limited self concept. Doesn't Mead's conception of the socially constructed self lead us to the conclusion that my "me-ness" has been learned, that I need not endorse its existence? The Japanese have a phrase "niju jinkaku." It signifies a person who is extremely changeable in character. I shall argue that we are all "niju jinkaku," that we change so much from situation to situation that it is an unnecessary distortion to label someone "neurotic," "hysteric," "courageous," "assertive," or the like without reference to specific situations in which these characteristics are manifest. (The description of the situation, including the behavior associated with that situation, is sufficient.) When character labels are applied without attention to circumstance we gratuitously circumscribe the attributes of individuals, we pigeonhole without adequate concern for process, change, shifting situations.

The title of this chapter comes from a Zen koan. It suggests the emptiness of the vessel we call "self." Beyond this level of understanding there may be said to be "no breeze and no bowl."

Eternal Stranger

I meet with him but don't know who he is.

I talk with him but don't know his name.

From *Zenrin Kushu* (An Anthology of Zen Phrases)

From situation to situation I notice different things, speak differently, and behave in a variety of incongruent styles. It can be argued that I am many persons. Only the name, some memories, some people, habits and objects seem to recur from setting to setting. My body changes. So do my memories and many habits. Certainly my perceptions of people and objects change with various angles and movements. There is a consistency of name, but it applies to this constantly changing flow of awareness I call "me." Even what I am called varies from place to place and role to role. Sometimes I am "Mr.", sometimes "Doctor", sometimes "*Sensei*", sometimes "David", and so forth.

Who am I then? This collage of identities, each pulled forth by situational context points to a changing self. It is but a small step further to the psychological Buddhist conclusion that I and the situational context are the same. There is only situation. Without the name with its spurious implication of continuity all that is sensed and all that is acted, all that is experienced and all that is recalled are contextually elicited and defined. My identity lies in the situation of this moment. I am the flow of thoughts, perceptions, and feelings of this situated now. In other words, there is nothing but this flow.

We have traveled a few paces beyond George Herbert Mead's "social self," but he was headed in this direction. Skinner, too, coming by a different route is finding that the locus for understanding human behavior lies in the setting and the constantly shifting behavioral history of the organism. All are abstractions from reality: setting, history, behavior, organism, identity, personality, self, me. All are changing constantly.

Gergen (1972) writes of the uselessness of the notion of one person-one identity. Goffman (1959) describes in intricate detail our social masks and wisely avoids inferring something beneath them. Deikman (reviewed by Goleman, 1976) is quoted,

"'There are so many varieties of you, moment by moment, state by state that only a very selective memory allows us the illusion of a constant, continuous self to be maintained.'" These ideas are not at all new. Psychological Buddhism has argued the bankruptcy of the notion of the single self for centuries. The Cartesian notion that "I think; therefore I am" assumes far too much. "Thinking occurs" is all that we can take as given. Even those words are abstracted symbols representing the process itself.

Following the line of thought above it can be seen the self-disclosing theorists like Carl Rogers and Sidney Jourard have made a fundamental mistake in assuming that there is some personality or self to disclose. Once I tell you something revealing about myself (of course, we select those aspects of ourselves we are willing to disclose) the theorists assume that the information I have communicated is relevant to understanding me in other contexts and at other times. This assumption is false. At minimum my self-disclosure changes me into someone different from the self I disclosed. At most I am a momentary-situation-person constructed (or abstracted, if you will) from a series of events that are themselves in flux. What I was yesterday (or one second ago) I am not now. In fact, as I reconstruct the history of this "self" I am constantly reinterpreting and reflecting it off the changing facets of current happenings. The material on Naikan psychotherapy below will elaborate on this reconstruction of one's history. My identity for the moment only forms as I ask myself questions like "What am I doing here?" "Why did I do that?" When I am lost in reading a book there is no "me." I have become the character in the novel. The flow of awareness has merged with the content of the story.

Most of this manuscript was written some forty years ago. Now, in 2015, as I read it (or as I read many of my earlier books) I do not recall writing it, the contents appear new, surprisingly interesting. "I" reflect that "I" could not write now as "I" did then.

Thus far I have used the term "I" out of convenience, despite its imprecision. Take this "I" to mean not some continuous entity, but a constantly emerging consciousness. "Aha!" you might say, "This 'I' certainly behaves with some predictability over time. Perhaps that predictability is all that we need to take from the concept of self. The predictability and continuity may not be directly experienced by the individual, but it may be observable by others over time."

"You mean to say that at this moment you are considering the concept of self in this way," I reply.

"Yes, and that is the way I considered it a few moments ago, too."

"That is the way you now recall considering it a few moments ago. You are now recalling. Or perhaps now you are no longer recalling but rather trying to make sense of what I am saying or perhaps...but the now slides by so swiftly."

Anthropologists began in the 1950's to seriously question two assumptions that had plagued their discipline since its inception. One was the assumption of uniformity--that people of a single culture shared common motivations and values. The second assumption was that of continuity--that preliterate people led lifestyles unchanged over the millennia. Both assumptions proved false under close examination. According to Wallace and Fogelson (1961) anthropologists shifted their efforts toward the organization of diversity, how it is that people with different perspectives and motivations can operate together in a sociocultural system. As anthropologists gathered diachronic materials on preliterate cultures, all of which were found to be changing, interest turned toward the conditions which fostered change and the multivariate effects of these conditions. Even the simplest cultures are neither homogeneous nor constant.

Parallel assumptions in psychology are now challenged in similar fashion. In the past many assumed a homogeneity to personality, a single self, uniform and measurable across situations. A more useful framework for understanding persons is to ask, "How can it be that there are so many 'me's,' yet I experience a sense of personal integration when I reflect upon the issue of the self." In other words, what is this organization of diversity in the individual?

Secondly, although psychology has been forced by clear evidence to recognize developmental differences in persons over time (at least up to adulthood; changes in the middle years of adulthood have received relatively little investigation), it has pretty much ignored the reality that I change from moment to moment, or, better, that experience changes continuously. Some important questions are: What stimulates this constant change in experience? How do these stimulants of change interact to produce the content and pace of change? And, again, how is it that I experience continuity over time despite my constantly renewing consciousness?

Psychologists might look to anthropology for clues about how to approach these problems in the study of the individual. Concerns with the foundations of ethnic identity during rapid cultural change exist in the literature, for example. However, anthropologists haven't been singularly successful in their explanatory forays. The answers to these puzzles are not simple. In the case of perceived continuity of identity in the individual important variables seem to be learned and shared orientations such as roles, memory apparatus, localized physical bodies, recurring social-physical settings, measuring devices such as clocks, and perceived spatial and temporal continuities in the physical world. Carlos Castaneda's fiction provides imaginative attempts to challenge and "disarrange" some of these continuity-supporting variables. They can provide heuristically useful information for the sort of studies I am suggesting will be important in the future.

This approach to understanding human existence allows for complete and harmonious integration of the social and physical sciences. The fields of psychology and sociology, for example, are distinguishable from each other when the organized continuity of the self is taken for granted. But both are subfields of what might be called identity research when the nature of the continuity and organization of the self per se is at issue.

A final point, in the urban world the awareness of our tenuous identities is particularly acute. Each day we meet many people who don't know who we are and so can't support our illusion of continuity. We try assiduously to cue others about our identities by selecting identity-appropriate clothes, cars, hangouts, speech, posture, foods, and mannerisms. We want others to recognize who we are so that they can respond appropriately and consistently and thus validate our self-concept. Continuity of recognition is one of the attractions of fame--the rock star and the eminent politician have assured themselves some stabilizing reflections of self in others' eyes.

Children are particularly vulnerable to attacks on their identities (see Rokeach, 1964), and respond with visible distress when we send them signals that they might not be who they take themselves to be. But adults, too, become disturbed when their identities are called into question. The accounts above of experiential researchers and others in the literature offer insights into the strains on identity when one even temporarily becomes another situated person. Take, for example, the case of a nurse who was assigned to spend one day in the role of psychiatric patient as a training experience. "Upon entering the ward the first thing that made me feel like a patient was the aide that unlocked the door when I rang the bell. The aide barred the doorway and looked at me as if to say 'Who in the heck do you think you are?'" Being mistaken is upsetting and challenging to one's sense of identity, being ignored altogether can have similar effects. Thirty minutes of being ignored by fellow patients for the day reduced another nurse in training to the following state: "I had the most awful urge to get up and run, not walk, to the nearest exit. If anyone had come up to me at that moment and said something--anything, I believe that I would have burst out crying--and I am not a 'weeping woman.'" Notice in the latter quote the desire of this nurse to maintain some continuity by describing herself as not being a "weeping woman." The reality in this situation was that she was a "weeping woman," or at least she was much moreso than in some of her more frequent situated identities. We covet the stability of the illusory, unchanging single set of personality characteristics to preserve the vision of the single self.

Experiential research demonstrates the fragile nature of identity and the dependency we have on others to sustain our identities for us. I have seen the effects of floods that washed away family photo albums and whole pasts. Like other anthropologists who have done fieldwork in non-Western cultures I have experienced the blows to my self concept as I bumbled along behaving in culturally-inappropriate ways. Who is this adult who doesn't know how to pay an electric bill, who hears the music of an ice cream wagon outside but sees a garbage truck, who runs excitedly up on tatami mats with his shoes on, who has difficulty getting about on a train system that children ride to and from school, who buys several pounds of an unfamiliar condiment which is ordinarily purchased in ounces, who must communicate on the level of a second or third grader, and who feels constantly visible and set apart by his physical features and strange behavior? My first year in Japan was remarkably instructive in teaching me about the cultural relativity of my momentary sense of competency and self worth. Then the experiential research in psychiatric settings described above further reinforced my awareness of the necessity of acknowledging our multiple identities. Despite the credit cards, degrees, love relationships, cars, houses, and other symbols of status and identity we accumulate to order and reconcile and stabilize our settings-of-action we cannot fully buttress the fragile latticework of identities we call the self.

It may well be that the major contribution of anthropology to our world has nothing to do with the findings of anthropological research or the theories underlying its investigation. Rather, anthropology has turned out professionals who have had to adapt themselves to awkward environs and situations, who have had to establish and maintain relationships with different and sometimes disagreeable people in order to collect data, who have isolated themselves from professional contact for extended periods during fieldwork, who have lived in positions of dependency upon strangers of all sorts for satisfaction of all sorts of needs, who have been required to translate and interpret actions meaningful in one cultural system into words meaningful in another. The doing of anthropology may be much more significant than the "scientific" results. Anthropology and anthropologists offer much to the beginning student of situated identity research.

Anthropology and Phenomenology.

Why do people behave as they do? Why is that nurse standing with her arm around the shoulder of that patient, now buttoning the patient's robe, now straightening her collar while the patient stands passively talking of her various bodily ailments? There are a number of ways to answer these questions about human behavior. Two traditional classes of answers have come from psychology and anthropology. The psychological explanation may include such elements as the individual perceptions of the nurse and patient, their psychological set, their motivation, their cognitive organization of the situation, their personal histories, previous learning experiences, memory functions, ego defenses, and emotional states. The anthropological explanation is more likely to concern itself with the shared symbolic meanings of some human aggregate. The individual nurse and patient are seen as representatives of categories of people who share a common culture and behave in culturally meaningful ways. This culture, in turn, is explained in terms of its history, environment (including other cultures), its psychological orientation (Benedict), and so forth. Both psychological and anthropological styles of explanation assume some pattern or fitting together of the explanatory variables and elements within the culture (anthropology) or the personality (psychology).

Attempts have been made to bridge these two styles of explanation. Concepts such as "role" with referents meaningful in both systems have been tried. The cultural system's role position and the individual role player provided a point of conjunction which allowed both for regularities of behavior and individual variation (see, for example, Shibutani (1955) and Goffman (1959)). Some anthropologists (Wallace (1961), Frake (1997), and Conklin (1955), for example) attempted in various ways to subsume culture within the cognitive functioning and content of individuals, in effect making anthropological explanations of behavior a specialized subcategory of psychology. My efforts as pulled together in this book can be seen as a similar enterprise. But rather than trying to find a meeting ground of common interest (such as role) or to subsume one discipline within the other I aim to incorporate both in a more fundamental exploration of situated selves.

My desire for a holistic approach springs in part from my anthropological background. Anthropology is a holistic discipline--or so we were taught. Archeologists, linguists, physical anthropologists, sociobiologists, cultural geneticists, ethnologists, ethnographers, and others are said to share a common intellectual foundation. This broad base of shared interests and training in a discipline that encompasses human culture, history, and biology, was once actually a real possibility. Now it is more or less a myth. Anthropology students have no hope of learning much beyond the surface of any anthropological subdiscipline. Even in the anthropologist's specialty, be it cultural anthropology or psychological anthropology or physical anthropology or whatever, much of the depth of understanding will come after the serious student has completed doctoral work and has begun operating as a professional. Only then is there the time available for reading and for research and for the effort to link concepts and theories with the young scholar's own fieldwork and teaching experience.

Anthropological education (like other social science education) is spotty not only because of the breadth of interest in the discipline, but also because of vogues and fads that sweep through ivy halls and motivate professors to offer students mere glimpses of depth in the field, spotlights of the teachers' current interests. These vogues reflect the lack of a unifying direction and base to the discipline, the efforts to succeed by presenting something "new", and the inability and disinterest in keeping up with a voluminous and scattered literature.

It is foolish to expect students to know everything about everything in anthropology. No one has that expectation these days. It is hopeless to call for a standard curriculum in this field with the breadth and variety of interests of its leaders. What may be possible, however, is a broad framework that shows how the pieces might fit together. Early anthropology, romantic anthropology, the anthropology of Ruth Benedict and Margaret Mead and even Radcliffe-Brown and Evans-Pritchard in their selective British way, considered culture to be "of a piece." All the elements of culture--from religion to economics, from social relations to subsistence, from art to law and politics--was seen to fit a single pattern. Everything functioned to support the whole.

As anthropology developed, however, it became clear that the "patterned whole" concept could be maintained only at the cost of ignoring a good bit of the real observable world. People behaved in ways that didn't fit the expected pattern, members of the same culture acted in contradictory ways, some cultures seemed to encompass strong internal pressures that were pulling them apart rather than contributing toward cohesion and continuity. Anthropologists came to realize that the lovely, aesthetic, simple view of culture-as-a-single-whole was artistic rather than scientific. It existed in the minds of the aesthetic anthropologists and not in the messier, contradictory world-out-there.

Understandably, this realization brought difficulties for the discipline. Nearly all the literature in anthropology (organized and interpreted field reports of observations of other peoples) was built around the notion of a single cultural totality for each of the tribes and bands and villages and nations studied. Could the literature be salvaged? Could the discipline be salvaged?

Several courses seemed to be open. One was to deny that preliterate peoples were anything but homogeneous. A few held that the modern world brought an unusual amount of contact with vastly different and civilized cultures, and these recent contacts muddied the waters of the earlier consistency and simplicity of native life. Such a course would salvage the early anthropological literature that painted a picture of primitive homogeneity and neat cultural patterns. But then what to do with more modern studies? Moreover, anthropology would need two sets of theories, one for, say, pre-colonial times and another for more recent periods. This course had obvious flaws.

Another course was to recognize anthropology as something other than science. Perhaps the discipline would be better considered an art form, one of the humanities, or some sort of hermeneutics aimed not at scientific proof but at interpretation. Such a course would salvage all the literature, all the history of anthropology, but it would abandon all the prestige associated with science and the big research money that goes with scientific endeavors in this society. Psychology faced a similar choice in the early twentieth century and elected to divorce itself as completely as possible from philosophy, jettisoning what was considered then part of its history for the sake of becoming a scientific pursuit. The success of that effort is still open to question.

Yet another course was the one that most anthropologists ultimately chose. That path was to make the discipline appear respectable scientifically. It required focusing on narrow problems, studying bits of culture in analytic detail, and paying only lip service to the hoary concept of cultures as integrated wholes. This alternative implied abandoning historical diffusionist emphases and turning to more theoretical and comparative studies. There emerged a whole new sophisticated form of anthropological enterprise in which the student avoided going to some remote village to live and study the natives. Instead the student pored through organized notes in a library, selected out categories of seemingly related behaviors from many different cultures, and performed statistical manipulations on ratings of these behaviors to see if they were correlated with other factors cross culturally. For example, some anthropologists looked at reports of child rearing in many cultures to see whether early weaning was related to subsistence type, religious beliefs, healing practices, and adult personality traits.

Again, a parallel development occurred in psychology. From the grand integrated theories of Freud, Jung, and the neo- Freudians have developed both the artist-educators of clinical psychology--literature salvaged, struggling for economic survival because they aren't "scientific" and the experimental psychologists--statistically sophisticated, analytic, and enjoying the status and grants due them in their scientific laboratories.

In both the disciplines of anthropology and psychology the development toward a more "scientific" appearing posture took the form of aiming to objectify the data to be manipulated and understood. Introspective accounts, phenomenological data became subordinate to the counting of observable facts--the number of bar presses of a rat, the correlation between population density and the occurrence of warfare, the percentage of "yes" replies to a fixed-choice question, the measurement of variation in fossil size and pottery decorations.

Criticism.

Not everyone is happy with the turn of events in these disciplines. Asch (1952) wrote: "Modern psychology has often drawn, I suspect, a caricature rather than a portrait of man. As a result it has introduced a grave gap between itself and the knowledge of man that observation gives us and from which investigation must start...We have a right to wonder whether this is not a spurious objectivity, whether it does not have its roots in a certain decadence and anti-human orientation for which the subject matter itself is not responsible, and whether the simplicity and apparent freedom from presuppositions may not hide a dogmatism all the more inflexible because it speaks in the name of science." (pp. 24-25)

Barker is an exceptional psychologist who has led a small movement in the study of ordinary life under natural conditions. He holds that "the science of psychology has no adequate knowledge of the psychologist-free environment of behavior." (1963, p.4)

Koch (1999) wrote "I want to make it plain that I think there to be an intense current need for particular analysis of many issues connected with the use of experiential variables in psychology. Experientialism--if I may substitute that word for the term 'phenomenology' which I dislike-- was driven underground in American psychology for almost forty years...There are, after all, open and important questions having to do with the relations between experience and 'report,' optimal techniques for experiential observation, prospects for methods of observer training which might increase the sharpness and reliability of experience-language...the formulation of adequate independent and dependent (experiential) variable categories, optimal modes for integrating behavioral and experiential data, and many others. These are no simple problems...the fate of psychology must be very much bound up with the progress toward their resolution." (p. 35)

Macleod (1965) contributes his insistence "that what, in the old, prescientific days, we used to call 'consciousness' still can and should be studied. Whether or not this kind of study may be called a science depends on our definition of the term. To be a scientist, in my opinion, is to have boundless curiosity tempered by discipline." (p.72)

It is, perhaps, not surprising that when psychologists begin to study human behavior in natural surroundings their endeavors begin to look like anthropological fieldwork. Braginski and Braginski (1969) proposed an alternate psychology of learning. "Thus, if the psychology of learning kept its phenomenological basis, then logic would dictate a redefinition of the area. Psychologists would...specify the content of the human experience in which they are interested." (p. 179) "Thus, we need psychologists who can become experts in studying the life space, the human situation, and the transactions between people, not 'learning' specialists who, by their own definitions, can only obscure and preclude the meaning of learning in human affairs." (p. 180) The example the Braginskis supply the reader for this new psychology of learning involves observation and interviewing within an elementary school classroom to get at what anthropologists would call the "folk" view of the schoolroom and the social transactions that occur within that setting. When the study involves human awareness and behavior in natural settings the psychologist, too, must turn to anthropological approaches and data. What else can be said about this discipline which seems to have cornered a large portion of the domain of naturalistic observation? What of anthropologists themselves?

The Anthropological Endeavor

What lengths anthropologists have gone to in order to learn the hidden lifeways of human cultures! What hitherto secret and barely-remembered customs and ceremonies have been dredged from the minds of half-willing informants! Different from psychiatry which seeks knowledge from the disturbed in order to effect change, anthropology seeks shared knowledge from the cognizant in order to comprehend. What physical discomfort, what social isolation, what risk to life and identity have anthropologists permitted in order to gain the acclaim of their small band of colleagues and to record sensible memorabilia.

A mad breed, perhaps, those who glide on such fluffy concepts as "culture," "tribes," "mazeways," and "social structure," who believe that humans are truly equal though gifted individually. Sometimes narrow minded in their resistance to muddling, greying change anthropologists react with head and heart in opposition to racist imprecision, to missions and colonialists and big business and militarists who want to "use" "their" people. Still children, these men and women, fret and quarrel among themselves in their departments and in their national meetings; they ignore the lesson of the fragile self that they once learned as simple-minded nuisances in someone else's culture; they jockey for power and security and student/disciples and money much as did others elsewhere (they understood and smiled with amusement at those others, though not yet at themselves). Anthropology, the regal head of the social sciences, a queen still served by child viziers.

When anthropologists began writing about the experience of fieldwork itself (e.g., Spindler, 1970) as well as the scholarly results of the fieldwork it became apparent that there were certain similarities between ethnographic fieldwork in another culture and brainwashing. Often working alone in some small preliterate group the anthropologist felt socially isolated-- geographically uprooted from familiar society and not assimilated into the unfamiliar one. Ritual debasement kept the fieldworker set off from others. Self esteem was attacked with resulting loss of confidence, increased self doubts, overconcern with avoiding errors and presenting a proper image. An alternate lifeway was taught to the reeling young graduate student/fieldworker. Obvious rewards were offered for adopting that lifeway--social recognition, praise, acceptance, and so forth. By the time that the period of fieldwork was over for some anthropologists there had been sufficient enculturation to make leaving the setting a painful, difficult process. Although the pressures that kept the student in the field differed from those in brainwashing during the Korean War, for example, the effects of isolation, indoctrination, and social acceptance for adopting another world view and lifeway were similar. Again, the lesson of the fragile ever-changing identity is clear in the traditional participant observation method of the anthropological enterprise itself.

Much of anthropology is listening, empathetic listening. It assumes that what someone (an informant) says about his or her world is meaningful. The listening may be preceded by structured questioning or it may not. The information heard may be coded into preconceived formal categories or it may not. But the essence is the careful listening to what another human has to say and an honoring of that utterance as important information. From this perspective anthropology is fundamentally related to psychotherapy, friendship, and other humanistic pursuits. Even the sorts of information attended to need not differ significantly from those attended to in these other endeavors.

The patterns and models of meaning which anthropologists impose on this information obtained from others in order to make of it "anthropologically useful" information vary somewhat from those employed by psychologists, psychiatrists, ministers, and others. The essence remains a human encounter, a learning. What we observe, what we test, what we feel and taste take on meaning in terms of what we have heard from those who have taught us--our parents, our peers, our mentors, our informants. When we failed to listen, we failed to understand.

Anthropology can be, should be an exchange. The anthropologist offers time, an ear, interest, respect, limited knowledge, and empathetic concern in exchange for information and other human satisfactions which the respondents are willing to provide. The chance to be heard may be eagerly accepted by some, grudgingly acknowledged by others, and ignored by yet others. Accepting responsibility to listen with attention is the sine qua non of any people-oriented human.

Some anthropologists have tried to systematize the data from what is heard in order to under and explain human behavior. The subdiscipline of ethnosemantics, for example, taps the verbal categories that help culture members organize their world. However, there are cognitive categorizations that are not only uncoded by the simple semantic symbols used in ethnosemantic analyses but that also lie outside of the culture members' awareness. What I am arguing is that formal analysis of verbal output cannot get at more than a small part of a reasonable understanding of human action and thought. For example, I would venture to say that in one American psychiatric facility with which I am familiar a woman who is wearing a pants suit can be predicted with great accuracy to be a nurse. Female patients don't wear pants suits. The nurse is not in a uniform (in fact, a great deal is made of the "fact" that patients and staff dress alike), but she is nevertheless identifiable by her dress. Thus, the formal dichotomy 'uniform--not uniform' may not distinguish 'nurse' from 'patient' on a semantic diagram even though one is likely to see systematic behavioral differences in hospital staff and patients as they approach an unknown female who is or is not wearing a pants suit. Put another way, while people are talking about dressing alike, they are ignoring real differences in dress.

Freud and others have discovered categorized semantic domains that their patients not only ignore but disavow, yet their patients' behavior clearly indicates cognitive interpenetration of, for example, semantically different terms such as 'father' and 'lover' or 'pain' and 'orgasm'. Would ethnosemanticists suggest that we banish from our understanding of cognitive functioning all those semantic and extra-semantic categorizations that our informants ignore or deny? Certainly, we must share some semantic categories or communication would be impossible. But the degree to which individuals ascribe idiosyncratic meanings to terms is probably higher than the formalized diagrams offered by ethnosemantic analysts would indicate. The degree to which we humans can communicate experiences, attitudes and feeling states is determined by a broad complex set of issues. We have a long way to go before we can make very useful any formal analysis of verbal output. Moreover, subtle meanings shift from situation to situation.

One of my concerns has been with making introspection respectable in anthropology. Of course, introspection maintained a closeted existence in this discipline since its earliest days. The reported memories of American Indian informants provided basic data for ethnographic reconstructions of tribal cultures that no longer existed when anthropologists got around to studying them. In anthropology the interest in folk interpretations and, more formally, folk taxonomies and other linguistic data rested on the verbalized accounts of inner structures. The fieldworker's introspective forays into his/her own psyche generated hypotheses and folk data, too, when the fieldworker was a culture member of the culture under study.

Yet in nearly every case the mental act of introspection wasn't acceptable in and of itself. It needed the guises of formal analysis by linguistic technique, numbers for computer manipulation, validation by archeological artifacts or psychological test measurements. Introspection was suspect--a poor relation of science kept in the closet but queried occasionally through the closet door.

The methods described in the suicide research above share the characteristic element of bringing introspection into each study as a key data gathering technique, valid in its own terms. As described above, the methods used in the study of psychiatric facilities involved immersion in alternate identities or roles already established in the settings so that the experiential researcher could become his or her own key informant. Of course, other data sources were also utilized, but these inputs were measured against my own experience as a participant in the systems. The research tactics are limited by my ability to initiate and maintain empathic contact (either with a specific individual in the case of live- alongside research, or with my conception of the alternate identity in the case of live-in research), by my abilities to conduct accurate introspection and observation, and by the unique nature of my experience that renders it inappropriate for generalization. My writing style is personal because the research about which I report is personal. I look forward to future comparative research generated by others who have carried out experiential research in similar and quite different settings from those discussed above

It should be noted here that one need not adopt another identity to do experiential research. Although the distancing and novelty of an alternate identity sensitizes us to events and objects to an extraordinary degree, there is no reason why we cannot apply experiential techniques to our ordinary identities. The oscillation between observer and interactor is possible within any context. One may begin by "locating" the context for the interaction. Where am I? What role am I occupying? Who else is in the setting? What are their roles? What is important about this setting? What stands out as figure against the taken- for-granted background? How do I fit with this circumstance of the moment? How am I part of the situation for the others in this setting?

One may shift the flow of attention to consideration of the historical time perspective. What brought us to this setting? What contacts have I had with these people in the past? What do I know of their backgrounds? What has been occurring in the recent past? Again, one may choose to direct flowing attention to current phenomena. What is happening now? What do these events mean to me? to the others? What is the impact of these present events on my psychological and social functioning? How are our roles and interactions fitting together now? What can I learn about myself and the others from what is happening right now? Such questions generate introspective, empathic understandings of life settings. They find support in symbolic interactionist thought that human behavior must be understood in terms of a self interpreting a situation.

Let me be specific. Why are you reading this book? Why am I writing it? Why will you sit or lie down while you read it rather than stand? Why did I pause after writing the last few words? These concrete questions about human behavior will find satisfying and complete answers only when we consider a self with a personal history (constantly in revision) interpreting a situation (constantly under evaluation). The next chapters show how the explanation can be further reduced to only situation. Science only deals with situations (when it tries to deal with self or personality it must situate and objectify them in order to make them subject to investigation and discourse); Buddhism arrives at the same primacy of situation, but arrived at by means of an introspective path. We consider next some lessons from two Japanese Buddhist-based psychotherapies, Morita Therapy and Naikan. What they imply about the self we shall find quite relevant to our analysis of the situated self, multiple identities, and appropriate methods for studying them.

Morita Psychotherapy: Dissolving the Self in Action

"A Harvard graduate told me not long ago of being in a class that was taught by a distinguished and revered professor. On the day a research paper was due, one of the students apologized for not having his paper ready. 'I was going to type it up last night,' he explained to the professor, 'but I wasn't feeling well.

"'You will find,' said the professor, 'that most of the world's work is accomplished by people who aren't feeling well.'" (Fixx, 1975)

It was in Japan that I first encountered the possibility that the form and content of research could be of a piece. It was not my idea, of course. The Morita therapists Kora and Suzuki insisted that life is a stream of experience and that experiential understanding ("*taiken*," literally, 'body-knowledge') would be necessary for me to fathom their methods. If I wanted to understand Morita therapy, they told me, it would be insufficient simply to observe the practice and ask questions as an outsider. It would be essential to experience it as a patient and, then, as a therapist. Only with this combination of experiences would I know what Morita therapy is about.

Because the concept of experiential knowledge was central to the study topic at hand, and, according to the experts, experiential knowledge of this therapy form could be gained only by experiencing it, there appeared to be no other recourse but to merge the content goal of my study with the method of studying it. I became a patient and, later, a therapist in addition to my anticipated role as anthropological observer. Rather to my surprise, what I derived from these two experienced role perspectives were some understandings different in quality and content from the understandings that were gleaned through more traditional anthropological fieldwork methods.

With these beginnings of my research in Morita therapy in the mid 1960's came the thrust and path of my research to the present. I think that most of my colleagues haven't recognized that the experiential research in suicide described above and the study of these Japanese Buddhist-based psychotherapies are of a piece. The content theme that ties the body of research together is that of personal identity. What/who am/are I/we? What is important about this "self?" Of what is it composed? How is its existence maintained or extinguished? Why would anyone want to extinguish this "self?" Both the research in American suicide and that in Japanese psychotherapy provide answers to these fundamentally human questions that are amazingly alike in many respects. Symbolic interactionism from the West and Buddhist psychological thought from the East offer perspectives on a set of truths that I have spent most of my professional life (and private life, too, for I can find no meaningful boundaries between the two these days) trying to fathom.

What is Morita psychotherapy and what light does it shed on these issues? Shoma Morita was a psychiatrist and Chairman of the Department of Neurology and Psychiatry of Jikei University, a major private medical school in Tokyo. His method for treating neuroses was developed around the turn of the century and continues to be practiced in Japan today. Morita called his therapy "field fox Zen" (*yako Zen*), a sort of rustic cousin of Zen Buddhism. He frequently used Zen phrases and concepts in his teaching. Teaching is the proper word here, I think, for however we may disguise it, psychotherapy is education. It is, perhaps, the finest kind of education-- that in which the teacher is engaged in a personalized communication process of exchanging information and adapting general principles to the individual needs of the client or patient. Morita called his therapy a form of re-education (*sai-kyoiku*).

In psychotherapy we teach such topics as: What is the nature of human beings? What are the fundamental causes of symptoms like tension, anxiety, fear, and shyness? What can be done to make life more satisfying? What is the best we can hope for by way of relief or cure? How do human lives interlock? and so forth. For a further examination of these and similar educational themes see London, 1964. We teach these topics whatever kind of therapy we engage in whether we intend to do so or not. We teach it by focusing on certain parts of a client's life for consideration and ignoring others, by assuming that early childhood is or is not important in treatment, by structuring who talks or touches in therapy and when and how and why.

Morita was aware of ideas from Western medical thought of his time; he knew the work of DuBois and Wier-Mitchell and Freud and the leaders of German medicine. But his thinking was strongly influenced by the indigenous Zen psychological system, not the religious practice of Zen Buddhism. Morita found that something like what Zen had to say about human suffering made sense in terms of his own neurotic past and in terms of the reports of his patients.

One might say that neurotic people are "experientially unrealistic." They want to resolve problems without facing them, without enduring the pain that accompanies confrontation. They seek inner solutions where direct activity is the only reasonable course open to them. They desire perfection from imperfect beings in an imperfect world. Moreover, they seem to be unaware that others face imperfections similar to their own and continue to get on about their lives. In a sense, neurotic persons are "self-focused." They process information about internal events, noticing their anxiety and self doubts and discomfort while missing much of what is happening in the world around them. For example, in one of our Morita therapy groups in Los Angeles a young man who had been attending the group for a couple of months arrived with his hands grimy from working on a car engine. When asked to wash them he walked around within the building searching for a lavatory. Two doors within the room of our group meeting were clearly marked "Restroom," and they had been used during group sessions. Yet he hadn't noticed them, so absorbed had he been in himself.

My American clients are instructed to note details from their "surroundings" (not the word I would wish for, it assumes a sort of person in the center surrounded by a situation rather than an interacting reality). Not only do they recognize more readily what reality has brought to be done by means of this directed attention, but they begin to pull their attention out from its strong overemphasis on that part of reality they call "me," and "myself."

The goal of Morita therapy is to pull the patient's attention into the broader world of reality. The patient is taught to lose himself in doing with care what reality brings to be done in each moment. Feelings are to be accepted as they are. Feelings are not to be ignored or suppressed, but they cannot be directly controlled by the will so there is no use struggling with them. Neurosis, then, is basically a problem of misdirected attention. Underlying that misdirected attention is a character problem, a set of habits of misplaced attention. And underlying that character problem is a fundamental problem of education. As indicated above, Morita saw that therapy lies more within the domain of education than medicine. How is this re-education accomplished?

Morita therapy is carried out in a variety of settings through a range of modalities. It is practiced in outpatient settings, in groups, by mail, through literature, and, in some cases, within various sorts of hospital settings. The inpatient Morita therapy is perhaps best known to Western readers although inpatient Morita therapy isn't practiced at all in the United States on a systematic basis and is practiced less in Japan today than it was forty years ago (Reynolds, 1976). Morita accepted patients into his home to live with his family and learn the practicalities of daily living. In time this practice developed into inpatient treatment in specialized hospitals. The first week of such treatment involves a period of quiet isolation. Less structured than the quiet sitting of zazen this period is called absolute bedrest (*zettai gajoku*). The patients are instructed to lie in bed for a week without talking to anyone, without reading, writing, listening to the radio, smoking, or otherwise distracting themselves from being alone with their thoughts. Three meals each day, one bath during the week, washing face and hands, brushing teeth, and toilet functions occupy them for only short periods of time during the week. The clients find no escape from themselves.

In the absolute bedrest of Morita's method there is no particular guidance, no question to ponder, no focus of meditation. The clients are told only to accept what comes into their minds. They are not to struggle with doubts or boredom. However pleasant or painful, they must continue to lie in place maintaining the simple regimen. The possible lessons to be learned during this period are many. Feelings float up and pass away. Thoughts appear out of nowhere, flash on the screen of the mind, and disappear into nowhere to be replaced by other thoughts. Pain and joy come and go while the behavior remains steady, one simply lies still. Some patients are cured of their symptoms by this week of structured behavior and unstructured experience. Most, however, go on to further weeks of task-oriented living with special diaries and lectures and individual sessions with a therapist. The above description of absolute bedrest is based not only on others' reports, but on my own experience of a week of absolute bedrest. The details of inpatient Morita psychotherapy may be found in Reynolds, 1976; here, however, I want to pursue some of the implications of Moritist thought for an understanding of the self.

Thoughts come and go. All we know is what is presenting to our awareness in this moment. All we are is this flowing awareness. When we think of the past we do so in the present. When we anticipate the future we do so in the present. This flowing now is all that there is. Even the flowing is inferred. Strictly speaking, this perspective implies that there are no neurotic persons, only neurotic moments or neurotic nows. This perspective further implies that, for example, depression which isn't being attended to in this moment is not a problem for the person in this moment. A "symptom," then, doesn't lie in latent menace somewhere until it appears. Rather it exists only when it fills consciousness with its discomfort. What a radically different perspective on neurosis and treatment and, more basically, the self we encounter here!

This patient is not a phobic person, he has phobic moments. Don't you have such moments, too? I do. We are not so different, then, though what precipitates our fears may vary and the frequency of fearful moments may differ. But the labels of being obsessive or phobic or anxious or hard-to-live-with or irritable or insane no longer make any sense from this point of view--they are too fixed, too lasting. The experience of these shifting thoughts and feelings turns our attention to the circumstances that appear to cause them. These situations including room and companion and physical body provide the occasion for this flowing awareness to pass along.

When Moritists advise their patients to notice what reality has brought them that needs to be done and to do it, they are suggesting a way of life that emphasizes situational focus and a sort of dissolution of the self in situation-presented behavior. "The task at hand" doesn't necessarily signify some work or chore to a Moritist. The task at hand may be daydreaming or swinging-the-bat-at-the-curve-ball or rereading the last paragraph or putting a book down for the moment. It is a sort of fitting or harmonizing what one is doing to the circumstances that life is presenting at this moment. The value lies not in accomplishing everything one sets out to do but in the process of doing itself. When one is attached to the result (a manuscript, for example) and the result is destroyed somehow (say, the manuscript was burned in an office fire) there may be no way to salvage the time and effort (one remembers in the now) that were involved. When the value is properly placed on the moment-by-moment value of writing the manuscript with full attention no matter what happens to the final product, the quality of the doing made the doing worthwhile. Similarly, Morita therapy offers the consolation (if that it be) that following any outcome, disaster or success, there is always something that reality has brought that needs to be done next.

The philosophy outlined here (and discussed in greater detail in Reynolds, 1983 and elsewhere) is not the sort of detachment and withdrawal from feelings that is associated with simpleminded understandings of Buddhism. It sees clearly that, for the most advanced yogi or the most mind-crippled hysteric, feelings appear and disappear and that understanding their source is unlikely to be of help unless that understanding leads to something that can be done (behavior) to modify the situation. Morita therapy is not ascetic. The Morita therapist Akihisa Kondo has called it epicurean--the way to taste the best fruits of life. I would call it eminently realistic and pragmatic. Morita's thought can be used as a steppingstone to mystic acceptance of "What Is." But it remains a comfortable location wherein one can find a lifetime of development without moving on at all beyond everyday reality. It offers a sure way of winning the game of life, and its definition of the game makes experiential sense to many. I have studied Moritist thought for fifty years now. In my opinion Morita was one of the greatest thinkers of his time. There is some narrowness to his writings, and some culturally conditioned sheer absurdity, or so it seems to me. But the depth is profound and the balance of practicality and theory at least equal to that of a Western therapist-thinker of about the same time named Freud (Reynolds and Yamamoto, 1972). Wisdom isn't necessarily original or exciting in some glamorous or mystical sense. Its chief characteristic is that it works.

The study of Morita therapy has helped Western therapists and scholars become more aware of some of our own assumptions, it has provided Westerners with another useful therapeutic mode (Reynolds, 1981, 1982), it has provided a reference point for useful and meaningful living, and perhaps it may help to stimulate a rethinking of the concept of the self in the social sciences.

The Buddhist base

Perhaps here would be a useful place to begin to fit together the Buddhist psychological thought underlying Morita therapy and Naikan (coming up in the next chapter) with Western notions of self. In the practice of Zen many people begin sitting as a meditative discipline in order to achieve enlightenment or satori. In time some of them come to see that they sit in order to sit. The case of Morita therapy is somewhat similar. Most patients come to be cured of their symptoms. They believe that involvement in the task at hand will save them by distracting them from their misery. As the tasks fill their awareness the suffering is crowded out at least some of the time. In time they come to learn a deeper life strategy, that is, to vacuum the floor in order to vacuum the floor, to wash the fork in order to wash the fork, and not with the purpose of trying to escape from their feelings.

N. Shinfuku (personal communication) has suggested that Buddhism is based on action rather than things or existence. Certainly the processual action orientation of Morita therapy fits that theme. It is the flow per se that is important (see Reynolds, 1980) along with the attention that is given to the punctuation of the flow by the "now" and the "me," or, better, the lack of such punctuation. Activity, however, isn't simply the physical activity of a "thing" moving through "space," but the "changingness" of which the movement of my body in working on some task is only one manifestation.

Conze (1951) provides the classic indication of Buddhist doctrine with regard to the self:
"The belief in a 'self' is considered by all Buddhists as an indispensable condition to the emergence of suffering. We conjure up such ideas as 'I' and 'mine,' and many most undesirable states result...The assertion that one can be really happy only after one is no longer there, is one of the dialectical paradoxes which to the man in the street must appear just as plain nonsense...The Buddhist sees it like this: Here is the idea of 'I,' a mere figment of the imagination, with nothing real to correspond to it. There are all sorts of processes going on in the world. Now I conjure up another figment of the imagination, the idea of 'belonging,' and come to the conclusion that some, not particularly well defined, portion of this world 'belongs' to that 'I,' or to 'me'...

"This step has an important corollary. If there is no such thing as a 'self,' there is also no such thing as a 'person.' For a 'person' is something which is organized round a supposed inner core, a central growing point, a 'self.'" (pp. 18-19)

Conze goes on to offer an illustration, based on the Abhidharma (which he calls "the oldest recorded psychology"), of a re-analysis of an ordinary experience in non person terms:

"Normally, one simply says 'I have a toothache." To Sariputra (the eminent interpreter of the Abhidharma) this would have appeared as a very unscientific way of speaking. Neither I, nor have, nor toothache are counted among the ultimate facts of existence...Impersonally, in terms of ultimate events, this experience is divided up into:

1. This here is the form, i.e. the tooth as matter;
2. There is a painful feeling;
3. There is a sight-, touch-, and pain- perception of the tooth;
4. There is by way of volitional reactions: resentment at pain, fear of possible consequences for future well-being, greed for physical well-being, etc.
5. There is consciousness,--an awareness of all this.
The 'I' of commonsense parlance has disappeared: it forms no part of this analysis." (pp. 107-108)

Conze goes on to point out that someone might argue that there is an imagined self as part of the experience. That imagined self would fall within the category of consciousness (5 above) as part of the content of awareness or as one of the volitional reactions called "wrong belief in self." I am not here interested in arguing the validity or utility of this particular form of analysis as contained in the Abhidharma; it is offered as an example of the possibility of an alternative sort of analysis which circumvents the everyday language employed in the human sciences-- a language which assumes the usefulness of concepts such as "self" and "person."

Herein lies the fundamental difference between this conception of the situated self and the Lewinian concept of life space. Kurt Lewin's field theory concept holds that behavior is best understood as a function of the person (p) and the perceived environment (e). These variables interact dynamically to produce the life space which is "the total psychological environment which the person experiences subjectively." (1935) The person was always at the center of Lewin's formulations. Lewin was criticized by some for failing to account for the objective environment in his formula. At any rate, the environmental variable was only utilized to help explain what was occurring in the psyche of this person-centered system. What I have suggested above as a paradigm for understanding my research in suicide, and what these Buddhist based psychotherapeutic systems seem to be confirming is the notion that the understanding comes when the explanation is not person-centered at all (that is our Western, humanistic bias). It must be the other way around. The truly centered explanation focuses on the environment with the person as nothing other than a part of the environment that we have abstracted out for study (as object) or for studying (as scientist) in this moment. The situated self is not merely an entity surrounded by this particular situation, rather the self is one aspect of the situation; it cannot be considered meaningfully extracted from the situation. Our focus is circumstance-oriented; the qualitative difference between situation and self has been removed. Although language requires some artificial constructions in order to avoid the appearance of awkwardness this perspective is properly process oriented. Watch the flow of your awareness. Phrases like "now walking" "now reading" "now considering" "now objecting" "now understanding" and so forth describe with some accuracy the flowing nature of awareness. Similarly accurate descriptions of what we abstract out of the flowing circumstance sound more awkward: "now chair-ing" "now sofa-ing" "now-'I'ing" "now book-ing." Our English language has separated out from the flow of circumstance certain elements to call objects (nouns) and certain elements to call actions (verbs), but all there is is flow. All there is is circumstance. Like the small human figure that blends into the scenery of an East Asian ink painting there is nothing but environment.

The symbolic interactionists have suggested ways in which this human fiction, the self, is created and what it implies in terms of thought and action:
"1) The possession of a self makes of the individual a society in miniature. That is, he may engage in interaction with himself just as two or more different individuals might. In the course of this interaction, he can come to view himself in a new way, thereby bringing about changes in himself.
"2) The ability to act toward oneself makes possible an inner experience which need not reach overt expression. That is, the individual, by virtue of having a self, is thereby endowed with the possibility of having a mental life: He can make indications to himself--which constitutes mind.
"3) The individual with a self is thereby enabled to direct and control his behavior. Instead of being subject to all impulses and stimuli directly playing upon him, the individual can check, guide, and organize his behavior. He is, then, not a mere passive agent." (Meltzer, 1964, p. 13)

It would appear here that Meltzer, representing symbolic interactionists, concurs with the Buddhist psychologists that the self is a socially constructed phenomenon. However, his third point that this self makes possible control and responsibility for behavior raises an important issue. Morita psychotherapy is built on taking responsibility for behavior while accepting feelings as they are. Morita therapy is Buddhist based, and so shares on some level the aim of dissolving the self. What sense does it make to dissolve the very self which makes possible the control of behavior? This apparent paradox, in slightly different form, is considered briefly in two of my previous books about Japanese psychotherapies (Reynolds, 1976, 1980). The standard Buddhist reply to this issue is that when the self disappears one's responsibility and compassion accordingly broadens to incorporate the whole of existence. Conze (1951) has put it this way:

"In other words, we should cultivate our emotions so that we feel with others as if they were ourselves. If we allow the virtue of compassion to grow in us, it will not occur to us to harm anyone else, any more than we willingly harm ourselves. It will be seen that in this way we diminish our sentiment and love of self by widening the boundaries of what we regard as ours. By inviting everybody's self to enter our own personality, we break down the barriers which separate us from others." (pp. 61-62)

Other Buddhists and Buddhist scholars have written very similar responses to this issue. It seems that in giving up the self one need not give up the functions of behavior control and responsibility, the construction of meaning, or even the locating of experiences in something identified as a self or a "me." The locating, however, is recognized to be a fiction abstracted from the flow of awareness.

We turn now to a method of therapy and personal growth which results in the expansion of the boundaries of the self along the lines recommended by Conze above. This method is called "Naikan."

NAIKAN: THE UNDESERVED SELF

That I can write about Naikan psychotherapy and its contributions to understanding situation and self is only in very small part a result of my own efforts. In countless ways I owe persons and forces recognized and unrecognized by me for this opportunity. The Naikan therapists and clients who talked with me, the founder of Naikan (Yoshimoto Ishin) who provided books and tapes and the chance to experience Naikan as client (*naikansha*) and then as guide (*shidosha*) for others, those who taught me the Japanese language, those mentors who contributed to my anthropological education, those who funded my research and fed me and clothed me and supported me in numberless ways--all these people made this chapter possible. Furthermore, as I have pointed out elsewhere, I cannot take credit even for these thoughts that are expressed here in print. For those ideas that came from printed words originated with someone else, and those that I had not read somewhere seemed to emerge from nowhere and bubble to the surface of my mind. I know not the origins of my thoughts at all. And the words I use were learned from parents and peers and teachers. To all these I am grateful (and sometimes forgetful of that gratitude). Feelings come and go.

This introduction to the chapter on Naikan was presented in Naikan style. From the perspective of this Japanese therapy form it is narrow-minded, and flatly incorrect for me to credit myself with authoring this book. The properly examined life will be lived in sacrifice for others, with humility and deep gratitude based on clear recognition of reality. What absurd pomposity it would be for me to be prideful of a body and mind nurtured through the efforts of others. If Morita therapy aims at eliminating the self through becoming one with the environment, by losing oneself in what needs to be done, Naikan achieves the same goal by demonstrating to the *naikansha* the myriads of ways in which the environment creates and sustains us. Like Morita therapy, Naikan aims to turn out realistic people.

Like all indigenous Japanese psychotherapies Naikan aims less at symptom reduction than at developing a character which overcomes the suffering medically called "symptoms". Developing character follows adoption and practice of a recommended lifeway. Why doesn't everyone naturally live in a Naikan way, with lives spent trying to begin to repay in some small measure what we owe our social world? The Naikan therapist points to two main reasons: avoidance and ignorance.

Avoidance occurs because on some level we fear to recognize this social debt. The fearsome vision of the burden we would feel, the guilt we would bear in realizing deeply that we have taken and taken since even before the moment of our births (from our mother's bloodstream) and have given so little in return causes us to close our eyes to the truth. Ignorance occurs because realization brings, in the end, not the suffocating guilt that we expect and fear, but soaring gratitude and, with it, fresh purpose in life. When we understand who we really are, according to Naikan thought, there will be no need for external prescriptions to do this or do that for others; rather, spontaneously and joyfully we will lose ourselves in the service of those around us, working on our debts.

The Naikan therapist holds that it is not sufficient for us to say, "Ah, yes, you are right. I owe a great debt to the world. I should strive to repay it." To do so would be to engage merely in superficial word play. To gain a genuine sense of the overwhelming nature of what we receive from others as contrasted with what little we return and what troubles we needlessly cause others it is necessary to examine our lives in great detail. This deeper understanding of Naikan truths comes through guided Naikan reflection. We consider now the practice of Naikan.

Simply put, in-patient Naikan (literally 'nai-' meaning "inner" and '- kan' meaning "observation;" the combination can be taken to mean "introspection") involves an initial week of intensive, guided recollection of one's past. In order to sample the method along with other naikansha I sat in my corner of a room behind a folded screen for one week from 5:30 a.m. until 9:00 p.m. each day reflecting on three themes: 1) how much I had received from, 2) how little I had returned to, and 3) how much difficulty and worry I had caused significant others in my life. The therapist guide came every hour or two to listen to a confession of my recollections and to assign the time period from my past and the person who would be the subject of my next period of recollecting. For example, we began with what I had received from, returned to, and done to cause trouble to my mother during the early period of my life up to elementary school. The next period covered the first few years of elementary school, and so on up to the present. Then I was instructed to begin again with the pre-school period, this time focusing on these themes with regard to my father and so on. The therapist always bows before and after each interview in recognition that he is not "better" than the naikansha and is prepared to listen without condemning judgment. There is no need for therapeutic interpretation during these interviews; the guide is present only to listen and answer questions and assist in deciding on the next topic for self-reflection. More detailed descriptions of the techniques and of my Naikan experience may be found in Reynolds (1977, 1980,

1983). Naikan is also carried out on an outpatient basis through journals, readings, and shorter (often weekend) periods of intensive Naikan supplementation.

Naikan shares with other Japanese therapy modes the themes of a structured family-like setting, a form of resocialization goal (basically, a Buddhist notion that when humans are properly educated about the consequences of their actions they will do good), experiential guidance by an authority figure, meditative format, de-emphasis of intellectual-rational knowledge alone, phenomenological focus, isolation periods interspersed with group activities (in Naikan there are group meetings during the week, notably at the end), the goal of symptom transcendence rather than symptom removal, key experiences during the fourth or fifth day of treatment, and loose enforcement of overtly strict rules. By considering the specific and concrete ways in which particular others have contributed to our lives in the past we begin to recognize current contributions not only of people but of other phenomena, as well.

For example, the clothes I wear and the chair I sit upon were created by others and distributed and sold to me by others. These objects help define the boundaries of my body. The electricity generated by the efforts of others makes possible the accomplishment of the typing of this manuscript. The sun's energy contributed to the growing of food that sustains me, and so on. A natural ecological perspective emerges as one considers the debt one owes to not only people but to electricity, water, one's car, and so forth. The desire to use these things carefully and gratefully wells up spontaneously during Naikan. The desire to repay one's car with servicing or one's telephone with a good cleaning or making one's bed in the morning as repayment for its support during a night's sleep doesn't appear unusual from this perspective. There is a sense in which the boundaries of the self begin to expand during Naikan. What is mine that I can call "me" when my body was given me by parents and grown by food prepared by others and my mind was nurtured by the teaching and writings of others and continues to be filled with thoughts that appear from nothingness? The question of when these gifts become "mine" (like the oxygen from the air, or the energy from the food) can find more or less clearly defined answers, but whether these answers are meaningful or useful is another issue.

Some Westerners who tried Naikan at the ToDo Institute in Los Angeles had characteristic complaints partway through their experience. They said, "I know I'm supposed to feel more grateful and guilty, but I don't. What is the matter?" It was necessary to explain to them that the basic purpose of Naikan is not to create some sort of feeling (remember, according to Morita therapy we have no direct control over our feelings in any case). The immediate purpose of Naikan is to generate more realistic memories of the past and more realistic perceptions of the present. For the reasons indicated above we all tend to be better at noticing and remembering what we have done for others and the ways others have caused us trouble. Naikan helps us remember what we have systematically misremembered and forgotten. Why is this remedial effort necessary? I suppose ultimately because it is best to be realistic and truthful and honest with ourselves. No one asks the *naikansha* to create a false cosmetic image of, say, a parent (though they sometimes do in a mistaken attempt to please their therapist guide). Yet, for most people, the result is a reconstructed view of the past and present, including their participation in the past and present.

Symbolic interactionists agree. "...Mead emphasizes how even past events are reconstructed, powerfully influencing the directions taken by present events." (Glaser and Strauss, 1964, p. 436) Strauss (1956, p. 328) points out that Mead recognized the ongoing revision of classificatory schemes as past experience is reconstructed and new objects arise. Certainly, the self concept is constantly being reconstructed in light of reconstructions of past experiences (quite powerfully so during Naikan) and in response to the responses of others. In fact, it is not only the responses of others which stimulate our reconstructions, but the response of our situation-moment with all its objects and energies and other constructs which has this effect on us.

Much of what I read in Sheldon Kopp's writings rings true. *If You Meet the Buddha on the Road, Kill Him* (Kopp, 1982), for example, contains much that reads like a sensitive blend of Morita therapy and psychoanalysis. However, there is a kind of forced Western independence to the lifeway Kopp recommends. This inattention to the ways we "are lived " (*ikasarete iru*) by our fellow humans and by the rest of our surroundings is, I think, a characteristic American blindness. Some Japanese and some Western graduates of Naikan have a firmer grasp on the interrelatedness of setting and self which makes some aspects of Kopp's view seem like those of a little boy shouting defiantly at the world "I'm going to do it all by myself!"

While Morita therapy developed from the thinking of Zen Buddhism, the religion and lifeway of the aristocracy, Naikan emerged from a subsect of Jodo Shinshu Buddhism, the religion of the masses in Japan. Morita therapy is cool with images of the stern father; Naikan is warm with prominent images of the encompassing mother. If Morita used the model of obsession to understand all neurosis (i.e., symptoms are attention distracted from the situational needs of everyday living), Yoshimoto considered all neurosis to be modeled after a character disorder, perhaps sociopathy. Naikan sees all humans as insufficiently sensitive to the contributions and needs of others around them. Following this rough typology a step further toward the West, it can be argued that Freud based his notion of neurosis on hysteria, a disorder for which insight is usually effective for immediate symptom relief. The Western love affair with rational understanding formed an appropriate ground for the Freudian raising of the intellect to therapeutic status.

What has the study of these Japanese therapies to offer the West? I looked at Morita therapy and Naikan and three other Japanese methods in *The Quiet Therapies* (Reynolds, 1980). There seem to be four benefits from their detailed consideration. First, they provide cases for testing our hypotheses about the relation between culture and psychotherapy. It has been fashionable to focus on the culturally embedded aspects of psychotherapies. On theoretical grounds some have argued against the usefulness of psychotherapies outside of their cultural contexts. Early on, Jacobsen and Berenberg (1952), Kumasaka (1965), Kelman (1960) and others considered Morita therapy inapplicable to Westerners because of its Eastern roots. Others were less clear about the cross-cultural applicability of Japanese psychotherapies, but they emphasized the cultural context in which they developed (Naka and Kawakita, 1964; Matsubara, 1973; Tatara, 1974; Smith, 1981). It is noteworthy that none of these writers practiced indigenous Japanese psychotherapies in Japan or elsewhere. By 1977 there appeared the first academic journal article (Reynolds and Kiefer, 1977) questioning the automatic dismissal of Morita therapy's applicability to Western clients on theoretical grounds.

There is evidence now that the practice of Naikan and Morita therapy can be usefully conducted in the United States. The focus for study shifts, then, from the possibility of application across cultures to the sorts of modifications and translations necessary to bridge the culture gaps. Constructive Living books (Reynolds (1984, 1986, 1987, 1989, 1990, 1991, 2002, etc.) aim to bridge the psychotherapy translation gap between Japan and the West. An intriguing sidelight is the subsequent modification of the practice of Morita therapy and Naikan in Japan as practitioners in the United States create successful innovations and introduce them back into the East.

The second benefit may be the opportunity for Western science theory building based on hints from the theories underlying these psychotherapies. For example, in *Naikan Psychotherapy* (1983) I outlined corollaries within Naikan of social exchange theory and Gouldner's (1960) norm of reciprocity. In brief, independently derived Naikan results seem to indicate that all humans default on the pan-human norm Gouldner postulates. Recognition of our failure to live up to this social norm may underlie shyness and stagefright. Another example, within *Naikan Psychotherapy* (1983) are supplements to symbolic interaction theory, self theory, and situational psychological theory based on the Buddhist psychological perspective supporting Morita therapy and Naikan.

A third benefit is that commonly found in the research of psychological anthropology. It is the capability of providing extreme and contrary cases for modifying culture-bound definitions and hypotheses. Much of what is considered psychological science today has been derived from observation and experimentation with undergraduate college students in the West. Freudian and neo-Freudian insights were derived almost exclusively from work with Western patients. Many of the definitions and models of psychology are, as a result, culture-bound. For example, from these Japanese psychotherapies we can derive a definition of psychotherapy that goes beyond (is broader than) the relief of neurotic suffering. Cure doesn't equal symptom elimination in either Morita therapy or Naikan. In the case of Morita therapy cure is doing what needs doing regardless of interfering feelings. In the case of Naikan cure is properly viewing one's debt to the world and working toward righting the balance; again, regardless of symptoms. In fact, symptom reduction or elimination is likely to occur in both these therapies, but such change is seen to be a mere side effect of the more important realistic perspective. The taken-for-granted assumptions of Western psychotherapy and psychology may be re-examined in light of these alternative strategies for personal growth.

A fourth contribution of the study of these therapies is that they provide viable alternatives for the practice of the art. In an era of some dissatisfaction with current therapeutic methods in the West, these methods for dealing with neurosis provide fresh perspectives and associated techniques.

NOTES FROM NOWHERE

I have included in this chapter some personal reflections about the research and thinking which has occupied me for the past fifty years. The topics are various, but perhaps the reader can find the thread of a message I wish to convey while you are doing me the favor of loaning me your attention.

On mental illness

For several periods of research I lived a good part of my life with those called "insane." Sometimes I was with them in order to treat them--but during the research I lived with them. I became part of their families, their institutions, their small communities. I lived with them in their violence and rage, their depression and their helplessness, their imaginative flights, their joys and tenderness. I was one of them-- seen by my keepers and by the surrounding neighbors as they are seen--handled, protected, despised, feared, ignored.

As a result of these shared life experiences I am impressed above all by the common humanness we all share with the mentally disturbed. I am struck by the patience, the sensitivity, the passivity of many of these blended-pressed-and-baked products of a life-recipe-ridden society. I am struck by their unwillingness to handle the grubby, phony reality that the sane endure and even learn to cherish. I don't idolize these escapees--many seem to have selected a lonely, selfish means of flight from their discomfort, exchanging for socially-consumed reality an essentially private view of the world. Yet I feel with them some of the suffering that is at the core of their attempted escape. In a sense, I remain one of their fellows. The best I can do for them is the same I can do for any human--to listen and try to understand what they have to teach me and, perhaps, to try to communicate to them (and to you) something of the way other individuals see the world.

The cause of much unnecessary human suffering in Japan as in America is the focus on the differences among humans. "I am not like you; you can't understand what I am going through," summarizes such an unfortunate attitude. When I see myself as like you in many ways, not only do I feel a bond between us, but also a tolerance for your actions and a sense that you, too, share some of my basic life problems. This recognition of our shared qualities is the foundation of humanism. It is also a fundamental element of the cure of neurosis. For as long as the neurotic person perceives himself/herself as suffering in a unique manner from a unique disorder, then ordinary methods of treatment aren't considered by that person to be applicable or effective.

Morita is said to have remarked that the young psychiatrists of his time looked only to diagnose the disorders of their patients. On the other hand, he made his diagnosis all the while looking for evidence that his patients weren't insane at all, and when he found normalcy he was relieved. How I wish that staff members in the psychiatric settings in which we carried out experiential research had held such an attitude! In only one setting was the cover of Kent blown by a perceptive and concerned manager in a family care unit for former psychiatric patients.

On psychotherapy

Essential to all psychotherapies are certain common elements. The therapists must communicate to their patients that they understand the patients' presenting problem. They may use evidence of their educational background, prediction of accompanying symptoms/disturbances, magic, personal qualities of empathy or other means to make their familiarity with the problem known to the patient.

All therapies create for the patient a meaningful past which led to the disturbance. They explain what happened that resulted in this current condition. This sanctioned past leads naturally to a current identity--one who is schizophrenic, one who is cursed, one who doesn't repent of his/her wrongs, one who is ignorantly living with misdirected attention, one who was fixated psychosexually by a traumatic childhood experience, and so forth. Any past created by a psychotherapy (or conceptualized on any basis) is fictitious. Meaningfulness is put into the creation of the past. The past created during therapy is not the past that the patient lived through moment by moment. In this sense the past that we devised for David Kent in our experiential research was no less real than the histories written in patients' charts in any psychiatric facility. Life doesn't organize itself into packages of psychotic breaks and curses and traumatic childhoods. The therapist must select from among past existences, experiences, identities to spin a meaningful tale for a patient's history.

Therapists must also communicate that they have a solution to the suffering client's problem. The solution most often involves effort on the part of the client.

This effort by the client is crucial to the success of therapy, and it provides the convenient excuse in the event of failure:

If you don't follow my directions carefully...

You must return to the clinic every week.

Don't fail to take three capsules daily.

You must believe.

Try this path diligently and see what happens.

Bring four eggs, a sacrificial chicken, and two gold pieces.

The client is usually instructed in what to do if the initial trials fail to provide the necessary help:

Come back in two weeks if this medicine doesn't seem to be working.

We'll approach a stronger deity if this prayer doesn't work.

Next week come with five eggs...

Implicit or explicit in all psychotherapies is the expectation of success. The elements of expectation and faith are well-treated in Frank (1961) and Kiev (1964).

On Diagnosis

The structure and content of diagnoses of psychopathology follow from the treatment modalities available. That is, humans come to define the nature of psychological problems on the basis of the ways they customarily treat them. It follows that cross culturally useful diagnostic categories will never come about until there is some agreement on proper treatment forms across cultures. Cross cultural studies seeking agreement on diagnoses such as those sponsored by the World Health Organization would do well to note this truth.

From the point of view presented above, the notion of a psychiatric diagnosis as it ordinarily occurs in Western medicine is flawed by a lack of attention to situational or environmental factors. A person labeled schizophrenic may behave and think in a perfectly normal way (as far as can be ascertained) at some times and places and yet hallucinate wildly at others. I am reminded of a schizophrenic acquaintance of mine who plays a strong game of chess and remains undefeated by checker players of average ability. His diagnosis remains fixed under both conditions of behavior. The permanence of a diagnosis also works to seduce the therapist trained in Western psychological science into ignoring the normal behavior that is appropriate within the abnormal setting of the psychiatric hospital.

I tend to look at most psychiatric disorders as "adjustment reactions." They are adjustments to people, places, chemical imbalances of the body, and so forth. To consider such adaptations "disease" is rather a strange conception, as many have pointed out (Szasz (1970), Braginsky and Braginsky (1969), and Laing (1969), for example).

The issue of diagnostic inflexibility becomes particularly apparent in the case of neurotics. Often there are clear situational pressures which call forth neurotic responses within a broadly normal life pattern. It is unnecessary to call a client's problem "a phobia" or "an anxiety reaction" when the person is at a given moment neither fearful nor anxious. Diagnosis fixes the client in a verbal shell that has only occasional reference to reality. Sometimes the compulsive handwasher does have dirty hands that need to be washed. However, speech in English and Japanese is ordinarily pruned to refer to types of people or character traits without reference to situational variables so that special conceptual and verbal training is necessary for those who which to speak about situated persons.

There is a stigmatizing effect of diagnostic categories in the field of mental health. Within the past twenty years or so we have seen a healthy progression in the delivery of services in the mental health fields in developed countries. We are moving toward community outreach with paraprofessionals and volunteers with specialty training. In the past we have had too many professionals doing too little at too great a cost.

Certainly, following major natural disasters we have seen the uselessness of professionals sitting behind desks in clinic offices waiting for those in need of help to present themselves for treatment. It is not unreasonable to assume that individuals in personal crises go undetected and unsupported in similar fashion.

I envision another step, however, more radical than any taken thus far. It involves mental health training for mental patients and others who appear for counseling and outpatient treatment. I mean here training in recognition of suicidality in others, counseling tactics, and broad interpersonal helping techniques. Such training would produce a reversal of orientation. The recipients of help would become service providers. They would develop skills useful to others in their families, neighborhoods, and hospital wards. Role relationships would shift from exclusive taking to more giving.

Training of children and prisoners in assertiveness skills and behavior modification has already begun movement in the direction of which I write. Success in those areas may help the professionals who currently see their clients as incompetent and unworthy of such training to reconstruct their perspectives of patients. Perhaps a new awakening may occur--a realization of the capabilities and potential of those diagnostically labeled "disturbed."

Thoughts on Anthropology

A well-known film director was invited to present a lecture about filmmaking at a major university. When he arrived the chairman of the program committee had several projectors and screens prepared, but there were no reels of film in the director's hands.

"Where is the film?" he was asked.

With a sweeping gesture of his arm the director's eyes traveled around the room, and he replied, "This is the film!"

He could "see" film all around--drama, comedy, romance, documentary. All were there in that room. He "saw" camera angles, entrances and exits, monologues and characters and climactic scenes. It was all there for the artist who could "see" the surroundings in this manner.

Anthropology is said to be the holistic study of human beings, and it is that. But it is also a way of looking at what is around us, a way that stresses connections: connections among people, between our physical animal nature and our cultural nature, between our prehistory and history and our present, between our language and our ways of thinking and acting, between our environment and our lifeways, connections among the patterned elements of our daily lives. Anthropological training provides skills in "seeing" in this fashion.

As I began my undergraduate study of anthropology I was possessed of the naive notion that I would come to know all that could be known about human beings. All of the strange customs, all of the religions and values and art forms from around the world would make sense to me in time, I thought. Knowing them, I would know myself. What foolishness! Reading the encyclopedic ethnographies of culture after culture becomes increasingly boring. If mere learning of cultural data were the task of anthropology, the pursuit would be empty as well as endless. Furthermore, the intellectual study of anthropology or psychology beyond a certain level helps my understanding of me hardly at all. Understanding in that intellectual sense alone has become increasingly unsatisfying, rather on the order of solving a chess problem or mathematical puzzle--just a pastime.

My theoretical knowledge of myself floats on probability and refutable hypotheses. My experiential knowledge, however, is grounded, certain, dependable in a more satisfying way. Such experiential understanding emerged from my doing, my observing, my reflecting, my having been; not so much from books or intellectual discourse except as those exchanges produced occasions for memorable events. What I am writing here is not anti-intellectual. I have invested much of my life in the intellectual understanding of humans, including myself. But there is a quality to life experienced that doesn't compare with life rationally interpreted. Scholarly analysis holds the possibility of enriching life-experience, but by itself it is merely an opaque template.

Perhaps the recognition of the value of experiential understanding underlies the mystique of fieldwork in cultural anthropology. Fifty years ago, a doctorate based on library research or even fieldwork within the United States didn't carry the same weight as one based on fieldwork outside this country. Fieldwork offers the opportunity to master certain skills and gain peculiar insights while obtaining materials for a publication. The social skills of the underdog may be learned experientially during fieldwork. Anthropologists may encounter cultures in which they are ignorant burdens to the culture members. They must develop relationships with the culture members so that they will be permitted to gather meaningful data, perhaps while they are learning the language. I carry painful memories of the embarrassing errors I made and troubles I caused Japanese colleagues and friends in the first days of my research in Morita psychotherapy. The anthropologist develops skills in observation and in time management within an environment of little or no supervision and guidance in the field. I recall naively expecting that all anthropologists would learn the humbling lesson that our self-confidence and status teeter on the fragile base of our cultural skills and social recognition in our networks. Living in the field with neither competence nor recognition by surrounding others should make such a lesson abundantly clear, I thought.

But anthropologists return from the field to write their papers and books. They re-enter their familiar social world, and, as has been elaborated in the thesis of this book, they become different persons again. They cannot return to the selves that they were before fieldwork, but they don't carry the fieldwork identities back to the classroom and conference either. The complexity of the data they saw and felt in the field becomes simplified as they apply word after word in single file to the printed page or course lecture. Furthermore, some anthropologists withdraw more and more from fieldwork as they progress up the ladder of academia.

There is an even greater tendency among psychologists for upper echelon researchers to remove themselves from the concrete levels of their data. Research assistants do the interviewing, secretaries type out transcripts of meetings, coders score protocols, and so forth. The senior investigator deals with the abstracted end products of these manipulations. Generalization and theory building are greatly facilitated by this distanced vantage point. The subtle variations and "wrinkles" in the data of human contact are ironed out by this intermediate processing. The results are theories that are useful in the assessment of processed data sets, but not nearly so useful in assessing human behavior in natural settings. One polar extreme in this unfortunate situation results in the highly technical statistical reports which rely heavily on elaborate manipulations of data and are so divorced from reality as to be useless. The value of such reports lies in the statistical innovations--gourmet cooking but no meal.

Anthropology has always been an amorphous, ambiguous undertaking. In most settings when I identified myself as an anthropologist those present took me to be some sort of archeologist or paleontologist. When that understanding was found to be mistaken in my case, it was often replaced by the image of a rather eccentric fellow with pith helmet and walking shorts who slips into the primitive forest to chart the ways of hidden tribes. Yet I work in psychiatric facilities in modern urban settings. Aha! you must be some sort of psychologist, they say. No, not a psychologist, or a sociologist, or anything else readily classifiable, though the formal degree remains in anthropology. Perhaps someday we shall have interdisciplinary departments of human studies with an experiential focus. Perhaps.

Reflections on a Television Interview

We sit before the cameras, casual, legs crossed. I feel a mixture of relaxed wholeness and fragmented tension--always a mixture, never one single definable feeling... the complicated changingness that is me. The interview begins, and almost immediately comes a strange question.

"Dr. Reynolds, we know that you have worked on a number of suicide research projects, and in one of them you got yourself into a mental hospital to study suicide from the inside. When you studied suicide as a researcher/patient were you really depressed?"

"More and more I keep running into questions that I can't find answers for; I find only more questions and puzzles and issues when I try to give some reply. It's as if you were asking me to point out where Jersey City is on the map, but I'm sitting here with a map of India.

"The first question I need to ask in return is what 'you' you are talking about when you ask 'Were you really depressed?' Your map seems to assume that there is some long-term 'me' that was David Kent, the researcher patient, and now sits here talking with you. That doesn't fit well with what I see on my map. I don't have a single personality, and you don't either, I think.

"We are different 'selves,' if you will, as we drive our cars, sit here talking, play tennis, sleep, ask for directions on the way to a theater, and so forth. I'm not talking about roles we occupy, but about some basic differences in each of us moment by moment. The continuity of a 'me' becomes an issue only when I (now) start reflecting back and call that David Kent 'me' and that fellow who drove to the studio today 'me,' and so on.

"But it seems that I'm drifting away with such talk. Back to your question. There were times when David Kent was genuinely depressed, but never only depressed. Feelings, in my experience, are dynamic mixes, never pure hues. Not only do they evolve over time, but they churn together in one instant. David Kent was depression in some moments--depression filled him, was him, but always in unrefined, murky form. Then when he stopped to see what was happening within himself, he stopped, and became analysis, not depression. If you are asking whether the depression was continuous over long periods of time the answer is 'no.'"

Perhaps it appears that in this conversation I am engaged in frivolous word games, playing with the interviewer. Perhaps what was said makes no sense at all or only trivial sense, or perhaps it seems to be the sort of abstract talk that only an academic would make--ungrounded in everyday reality, a cloud passing by an ivory tower. I assure you that the intent of the conversation was serious, and that it makes sense in terms of my everyday life, and, I suspect, in terms of yours, as well. This book is about what sense it does make.

To help the reader see how these notions are grounded in my view of reality I have written this strange sort of intellectual autobiography. The content of the writing jumps back and forth between some personal experiences and theoretical understandings, between scientific research and a personal quest. My quest has led me through Buddhist monasteries in Japan and psychiatric hospitals in the United States, through disaster sites and nursing homes. Research has caused me to live with families other than my own, alongside discharged mental patients in aftercare facilities, in temples and in tents. What others have taught me caused me to rethink much of what I took for granted. Always changing.

Hidden Values of Research

Traditional methods of behavioral science research sometimes involve exploitation of the subjects studied. The exploitation may be justified in terms of token payments to the informants, course credit (as in some introductory psychology classes), or in terms of the potential benefit the research findings might have for the subjects specifically or for humanity in general.

Here I wish to consider some research methods that have the potential of providing important services to the subjects in the course of the research itself. In other words, regardless of formal payments or hazy future possibilities these methods offer the subjects satisfactions as an immediate benefit from the interaction involved—no-learn-now-pay later arrangement for the investigator/subject; it is pay as you go. The classic model for these ordinary research methods is psychotherapy. In order to be of benefit to his or her clients the psychotherapist must learn from them.

In the course of research on death and grieving among Los Angeles ethnic groups (Kalish and Reynolds, 1973, 1976, 1977; Reynolds and Kalish, 1974a, 1974b) and on self destructive behavior among elderly nursing home residents (Reynolds and Nelson, 1981) I conducted a number of interviews with dying persons in hospital and nursing care facilities. These dying humans were in the unique circumstance of having some rough idea of the likely period of life remaining to them. They faced the same human predicament of mortality which faces each of us. They were dying. So are we all. They were my teachers.

Much of our behavior can be seen as a flight from facing the inevitability of personal death. Becker (1973) has written perceptively on this subject. Dying people may have more trouble avoiding serious consideration of death. There are cues that keep reminding them of what is happening to their bodies. To be sure, despite all these reminders some patients do ignore or deny the inevitable. But for many of them come thoughts of how life was spent, how loved ones will carry on, how the last few days will be passed, how the grand enigma will be faced. Why am I here? How will it be without me? What changes lie ahead of me?

One of the personal benefits of research in dying and grieving is that such questions are posed again and again for the researcher. The researcher, too, can evade these issues, but it is more difficult to do so in these research settings. Among those researchers whom I know in this field of study are some of the liveliest in my acquaintance. Perhaps the surrounding symbols of finitude spur us to living fully within our own measured days.

The special circumstance of dying persons includes the high probability that they have only a limited period of time in which to ponder these vital issues and only limited capacities to effect changes in the world in order to redress past errors or omissions. With physical limitations all that is possible for many (beyond basic physical functions) is thinking and talking. What many patients seem to need is information for meaningful thought and a listener for meaningful talk. Of course, there may be needs for specialized physical care, pain medication and the like, as well. The interview process can provide the dying patient with the opportunity to consider and express thoughts about whatever is on his or her mind. Staff may offer sensitive listening, but staff members have other duties and time constraints. The research interviewer may not have a background in psychotherapy, but there seems to be value in the attentive listening itself. The Naikan admonition to treasure the words that we hear, else we are "stealing" them from the speaker underscores the potential import of interviewing in these settings.

Not only on wards for the dying but in suicide prevention and other crisis intervention circumstances, during psychotherapy, in negotiations with prisoners and terrorists, and in the conduct of participant observation and experiential research the sensitive, listening ear is of key importance. Those with whom we work need to be heard. To be permitted to conduct our work while providing the service of listening is a special privilege.

In our study of Black Americans, Japanese Americans, Mexican Americans, and Caucasian Americans in the Los Angeles area we conducted interviews lasting over an hour on the sensitive topic of death. Using a quota sampling method we obtained interviews from about equal representatives of three age groups and both sexes in comparable economic strata from the community. The 178 questions included:

How many persons that you knew personally died in the past two years?

How often have you visited someone's grave, other than during a burial service, during the past two years?

About how often do you think about your own death?

If you were dying would you want to be told?

Have you ever felt that you were close to dying?

Have you seriously talked with anyone about your experiencing death someday?

How do you know when someone is not grieving normally and needs help?

Have you ever experienced or felt the presence of anyone after he had died?

How would you like your body to be disposed of?

At what age do you expect to die?

Despite the nature of these sensitive questions, about three out of five qualified respondents agreed to be interviewed. And when the interview was completed only about one in ten interviewees reported that they believed the interview had a negative effect on them. Four out of ten reported a positive effect from the interview. Many of those who reported a positive effect said that the questions caused them to consider issues and possibilities that needed to be looked at in their lives.

In addition to opening the possibility for communication about a socially taboo topic the structure of the interview indicated connections between topics; it organized subtopics in a characteristic way. When an interview is conducted it has the potential for teaching the informant about the way the interviewer is organizing his/her view of the world. Our interviewers were members of the ethnic groups interviewed and, though well-trained, were not professional counselors. Yet during the human contact of the research setting they had the opportunity to offer expressions of sympathy, to hear outpourings of personal problems, and to thank the respondent for the valued information provided. The interview was both a personal encounter and an educational tool. The interviewees could learn from the interview itself that these topics could be looked at in an orderly way, that someone finds such an organization of the information desirable, and that they could "fit" their knowledge into this orderly framework. Without demanding any commitment or agreement from the respondents we were able to present them with new perspectives on these issues, alternative courses of action they may not have considered previously, and skilled listening even beyond the scope of the interview topics.

There was nothing particularly meritorious about our research in this regard. Many projects involving questionnaires, interviewing, participant observation and other research methods offer similar returns to the subjects under study. I only wish to point out here that the process of gathering information need not be considered simply exploitation of the voluntary subject. Some advantages for subject and for researcher are not immediately apparent.

Experiential Research in a Nursing Home.

In 1973 Adshead wrote a prizewinning dissertation at the University of Southern California based on his experiential research as a patient in a nursing home. Adshead lived for thirty-one days in a convalescent hospital. His identity was known to two administrators but not to staff. His dissertation provides an important resource for materials on theory, rationale, documentation, and preparations for this style of research. Adshead offers sound advice to the prospective experiential researcher. He advises that one undertake such a study not merely for the excitement and novelty of the approach, but rather because what needs to be learned requires this methodology. He suggests that researchers with experience in this methodology be consulted prior to undertaking a study. For this reason, I was invited to sit on Adshead's doctoral committee. "Finally, you can expect major changes in the behavioral and experiential "you" as you work through the method and anticipate the experience, especially if the research milieu is as different to you as mine was to me. You will not only behave and experience phenomena at entirely different levels, but will also run the risk of jeopardizing close personal relationships..." (Adshead, 1973, p. 50)

To provide the reader with some sense of the content of Adshead's findings I have included short quotes from his journal record:

(Seventh Day)
"Experientially, nothing's happening, nothing new, stimulating, different. Haven't thought a "big" thought since the second day. No thoughts of international problems, organizations, world affairs,...nothing. Here, experiential time stops, and chronological time dominates. So thoughts cycle back through past memories, past experiences, and forward only to predictable events such as meals and showers. There are no vertical experiences; all is isolation, deadenedness (sic) coming together." (p. 90)
(Second Day)

"The comedy-tragedy of existence here last night overwhelmed me. The sounds of misery, physical and mental discomfort constitute the night's experiences. A woman calling out in the dark, 'Teacher...teacher...oh, teacher, where are you? I'm here and ready...Mother...Mother...Mother...oh, Mother help me! I don't know what to do and I can't do it. Uncle...oh Uncle, what shall I do?' Then, a male patient calls out in anger to her, saying, 'Oh, shut up your goddamn mouth, you stupid old woman. Nurse tell her to shut the hell up.' (The nurse does not respond.) The woman continues calling out. The old man again calls out and finally gets an aide to shut his door so he won't hear the woman's cries. E. says, 'You'd think she'd [the nurse] try to calm her [the crying woman] down so she doesn't disturb everybody else, wouldn't you? Stupid sons-a-bitches! They're stupid bastards on the night shift.'" (p. 269)

Adshead also includes a brief account of his debriefing with the staff following the live-in phase of the study, and he offers specific and general suggestions for restructuring nursing care facilities into more human supporting systems.

THE SITUATED SELF

From my first years in college my mind was filled with questions about the definitions and boundaries of academic disciplines. Why did psychology ignore the psyche--that flow of awareness which is my mind? How could there be a boundary between psychology and cultural anthropology--didn't each presuppose and fulfill the other? How could economics or politics or history make sense without knowledge of the ways humans think and behave? Were Freud's psychological insights from the Vienna of 1910 to be considered history or psychology or cultural anthropology? Even mathematics made more sense to me as I understood the historical and cultural context in which the ideas occurred. And the artificial fences between anthropology and sociology sometimes made even my professors wince in discomfort.

It makes no difference in what disciplinary camp, if any, the ideas in this book appear as residents. It took me until I was nearly forty to realize that, in a peculiar sense, novelists were dealing with the reality of human life and scientists with a kind of fiction. Until then I thought it was the other way around. When the realization came I was relieved that anthropology remained a curious discipline straddling the hazy boundary between science and art. I wasn't required to teach the shadowy near truths of GNP's and learning curves and diagnostic categories and historical events. I was permitted to try to put into words what I saw and felt in my lives in Japan and elsewhere.

For the longest time I told the safe, scientific part-truths as I had been taught to do, while only hinting at the patterns I could sense were in the world but wasn't wise enough to be able to demonstrate with acceptable forms of scientific data. The small segments of that Larger Truth which seemed understandable at times (with effort and experience and long thought) couldn't be passed along directly in my writings. Like others I was forced to disguise, cram, and conceal what I believed to be true within the undergarments of Science in order to make respectable presentations. For better or for worse, this book bares more of my worldview than any academic work I have written.

Looking back I am somewhat surprised to see a set of suppositions about morality and efficiency surfacing from this body of scientific research. My dissertation contrasted Morita psychotherapy with brainwashing. One conclusion was that brainwashing is less effective because the subjects are not willing volunteers. The brainwashing captor must spend time and energy insuring that the captive doesn't escape from the setting or otherwise act to sabotage the arrangements for inducing change. With a cooperating volunteer (as are some patients in psychotherapy) the change agent can devote more effort to producing the desired change without being sidetracked by the spurious struggle to maintain the integrity of the setting.

Similarly, in the research on suicides in hospitals Farberow and I concluded that humane treatment of psychiatric patients by staff would probably reduce suicides and ease the staff's workload--a workload which varies considerably according to the cooperativeness of the patients. Again, in psychiatric aftercare facilities and nursing care facilities simple acts of courtesy and human concern by staff were likely to reduce self destructive and other disordered behavior among the residents.

On terminal care wards and nursing care wards the quality of patient care seemed to influence the life satisfaction of the patients which, in turn, seemed to be related to how long the patients lived and the amount of self-injurious behavior they displayed, even holding constant the type and severity of illness. The usefulness of such research, I believe, lies in the detailed descriptions of the ways in which human concern is or is not expressed among persons and suggestions about the probable consequences of different styles of relating. The concept of value-free scientific discourse has become considerably narrowed in the process, however.

There is truth and there is truth. The kind of truth that requires me to recite statistics on suicides in various countries or to count the number of practitioners of Morita therapy in Japan today and not miscount by so much as one person isn't very exciting. This is not to say that such truth is unimportant or that it is necessarily trivial. It is just that it is of relatively little interest to me. The kind of truth I find worth teaching, for example, is that which helps my students see themselves as, in some human ways, persons like mental hospital patients whose power and independence are sucked from them by the situational pressures of some huge institution--an institution which operates more for the convenience of administration and staff. Similarly, faculty can see themselves as, in some human ways, persons like mental patients in a psychiatric ward that is run for the convenience of administration. That truth is only a part truth. It is not all of what a university is, in the sense that forty-six may be the complete answer to the question of how many Morita therapists were practicing in Japan in 1975. But it is a part truth worthy of our attention.

Summary

What characterizes the theoretical orientation of the research described in this book? Firstly, change is taken as given. There is only flux, so it is the flux itself that must be studied. Static descriptions and models may be used only with the explicit understanding that they are abstracted from the reality of change.

Secondly, ideas are recognized to be situationally couched. Whether they are the ideas of scientific theory or the ideas of the informant or the researcher of the moment they find their meaning in the situational context of the ongoing moment. In this phenomenological sense, scientific truth must be rediscovered or reinterpreted again and again as it comes into awareness.

Thirdly, all research is researcher-included research. All research is based at some level on observation, interpretation, decisions concerning what data to consider and what data to ignore. Whatever elements of objectivity there may be come from multiple subjective comparisons. The research methods of experiential research and shadowing explicitly utilize the subjective element through incorporation of introspectively obtained data.

Fourthly, the body of research presented makes no claim to being value-free. The moral and ethical nature of any study of the human condition is considered fundamental. The responsibility of the investigator is to make public those purposes and values within his/her awareness which will have probable effects on the data when reporting research results.

Fifthly, the distinction between theoretical and applied research is seen to be unrealistic. All research is, in a sense, applied research. At minimum, all research changes the researcher. Knowledge changes systems. All research has practical consequences for someone.

Sixthly, a specific suggestion for theory development grew from the historical roots of symbolic interaction and psychological Buddhism. Presented initially in its conservative form, the theory holds that situational determinants cannot be ignored when attempting to understand/explain human behavior. A variety of examples are presented in this book to demonstrate that what may appear to be exotic or "crazy" behavior can be seen to be understandable and even rational when the situational context of the behavior is taken into account. In its most extreme form the theoretical argument holds that personality or self variables are socially derived fictional constructs that are unnecessary in the explanation of human conduct--that characterological variables can be subsumed within the situational context, which alone offers sufficient explanatory power.

Following the theoretical line presented here it would follow that the reader's acceptance or rejection of the theory of the situated self and the method of experiential research would be determined by the context in which the reader is operating at this moment. Those readers who have been operating within another theory and style of research are likely to look with a more critical eye at the formulations put forth above. Those readers currently exploring alternative styles of research and theory are more likely to flesh out the skeletal arguments above with supporting notions of their own. There is no need to posit long term personality variables along the lines of conservative/liberal, introverted/extroverted, inner-directed/outer-directed, and the like. Analysis of the ongoing situational context in which the arguments are being considered would provide sufficient understanding of the shifting nature or constancy of attitude toward this theory.

Admittedly, the analysis of situational context (including the ever-changing flow of awareness which is part of that context) is a difficult undertaking requiring great sensitivity and no little effort. Only the first steps in situational analyses have been made. Much further development in theory and method will be required before a convincing and acceptable case can be made for extending science in the direction of the study of situated selves. I believe that the results will be worth that effort.

References

Asch, Solomon E. *Social Psychology*. Prentice Hall, Englewood Cliffs, 1952.

Adshead, Francis L. Patient life in a nursing home: An experiential study. Dissertation U.S.C., 1973. *Dissertation Abstracts International*, 4467-4468, 1974.

Beck, Aaron T. *Depression: clinical, experimental, and theoretical aspects.* Harper and Row (New York), 1967.

Becker, Ernest. *The Denial of Death*. Free Press, 1973.

Bem, Daryl J. In Magnusson, David. *Toward a Psychology of Situations: an Interactional Perspective.* Erlbaum, Hillsdale, N.J., 1981.

Benedict, Ruth. *Patterns of Culture*. Houghton Mifflin, New York, 1934, 1961.

Blumer, Herbert. "Society as Symbolic Interaction". In Arnold M. Rose. *Human Behavior and Social Process: An Interactionist Approach*. Houghton-Mifflin, 1962. Reprinted in Blumer (1969).

Barker, R. *The Stream of Behavior*. Appleton, Century, Crofts, New York, 1963.

Blumer, Herbert (1969). *Symbolic Interactionism. Perspective and Method.* Berkeley: University of California Press.

Bowers, Kenneth S. In Magnusson, David. *Toward a Psychology of Situations: an Interactional Perspective.* Erlbaum, Hillsdale, N.J., 1981.

Braginski, Benjamin M., Dorothea D. Braginski, Kenneth Ring. *Methods of Madness.* Holt, Rinehart, and Winston, 1969 (paperback, 1974).

Cantor, Nancy. In Magnusson, David. *Toward a Psychology of Situations: an Interactional Perspective.* Erlbaum, Hillsdale, N.J., 1981.

Conklin, Harold C. Hanunoo color categories. *Southwestern Journal of Anthropology* 11(4), 339-344, 1955.

Conze, E. *Buddhism: Its Essence and Development.* Oxford University Press, 1951.

Deane, William N. The reactions of a nonpatient to a stay on a mental hospital ward. *Paychiatry*, 24(1), 61-68, 1961.

Edgerton, Robert B.and Bercovici, Sylvia M. The cloak of competence: Years later. *American Journal of Mental Deficiency* 80(5), 485-497, 1976.

Farberow, Norman L. and Reynolds, David K. Dyadic crisis suicides in mental hospital patients. *Journal of Abnormal Psychology*, 78(1), 77-85, 1971.

Fixx, James F. Sooner or later. *Juris doctor* (5), p. 68, 1975.

Frake, Charles O. Plying frames can be dangerous. In *Mind, Culture, and Activity*. Cole, Michael et al. Cambridge University, 1997.

Frank, Jerome. *Persuasion and Healing.* Johns Hopkins University, Baltimore, 1961.

Gergen, K.J. The healthy, happy human wears many masks. *Psychology Today*, 31-35, 64-66, 1972.

Glaser, Barney G. and Anselm Strauss. *Awareness of Dying.* Aldine, Chicago, 1965.

Goffman, Erving. *The Presentation of Self in Everyday Life.* Doubleday, New York, 1959.

Gouldner, Alvin W. The norm of reciprocity: A preliminary statement. *American Sociological Review* 25(2), 161-178, 1960.

Howard, Alan. Interactional psychology: Some implications for psychological anthropology. *American Anthropologist* 84(1), 37-57, 1982)

Ions, Edmund. *Against Behaviouralism.* Oxford: Basil Blackwell, 1977.

Iwai, Hiroshi and Reynolds, David K. Morita therapy: The views from the West. *American Journal of Psychiatry,* 126(7), 1031-1036, 1970.

Kalish, Richard A. and Reynolds, David K. Phenomenological reality and postdeath contact. *Journal for the Scientific Study of Religion,* 12, 209-221, 1973.

Kalish, Richard A. and Reynolds, David K. *Death and Ethnicity: A Psychocultural Study*. Los Angeles:University of Southern California Press, 1976.

Kalish, Richard A., Reynolds, David K., and Farberow, Norman L. Community attitudes toward suicide. *Community Mental Health Journal*, 10(3), 301-308,1974.

Kiev, Ari. *Magic, Faith, and Healing*. Free Press, Glencoe, 1964.

Koch, Sigmund et al. *Psychology in Human Context*. University of Chicago Press, 1999.

Kopp, Sheldon B. *If You Meet the Buddha on the Road, Kill Him*. Bantam, 1982.

Laing, R.D. *The Divided Self*. Random House, 1969.

Lewin, Kurt. *A Dynamic Theory of Personality*. McGraw-Hill, New York, 1935.

Macleod, R.B. Phenomenology: A challenge to experimental psychology. In *Behaviorism and Phenomenology. Contrasting Bases for Modern Psychology*. Wann, T.W.et al. University of Chicago Press, 1965.

Mead, George H. *Mind, self and society*. Univ. of Chicago Press, 1934.

Magnusson, David. *Toward a Psychology of Situations: an Interactional Perspective*. Erlbaum, Hillsdale, N.J., 1981.

Ohara, Kenshiro and Reynolds, David K. Changing methods in Morita psychotherapy. *International Journal of Social Psychiatry*, 14(4), 305-310, 1968.

Reynolds, David K. *Morita Psychotherapy*. Berkeley:University of California Press, 1976.

Reynolds, David K. *The Quiet Therapies*. Honolulu:University Press of Hawaii, 1980.

Reynolds, David K. and Farberow, Norman L. *The Family Shadow: Sources of Suicide and Schizophrenia*. Berkeley:University of California Press, 1981.

Reynolds, David K. *Naikan Psychotherapy: Meditation for Self Development*. Chicago:University of Chicago Press,1983.

Reynolds, David K. *Constructive Living.* Honolulu:University of Hawaii Press, 1984.

Reynolds, David K. *Playing Ball on Running Water.* New York:Morrow, 1984.

Reynolds, David K. *Even in Summer the Ice Doesn't Melt.* New York:Morrow, 1986.

Reynolds, David K. *Water Bears No Scars.* New York: Morrow, 1987.

Reynolds, David K. *Pools of Lodging for the Moon.* New York: Morrow, 1989.

Reynolds, David K. *Flowing Bridges, Quiet Waters.* Albany: SUNY Press, 1989.

Reynolds, David K. *A Thousand Waves.* New York: Morrow, 1990.

Reynolds, David K. *Thirsty, Swimming in the Lake.* New York: Morrow, 1991.

Reynolds, David K. *Rainbow Rising from a Stream.* New York: Morrow, 1992.

Reynolds, David K., ed. *Plunging Through the Clouds.* Albany: SUNY Press, 1993.

Reynolds, David K. *A Handbook for Constructive Living.* New York: Morrow, 1996, University of Hawaii Press, 2002.

Reynolds, David K. *Water, Snow, Water.* University of Hawaii Press, 2013.

Reynolds, David K. On Being Natural: Two Japanese Approaches to Healing. In Sheikh, A. A. and Sheikh, K. S., eds. *Eastern and Western Approaches to Healing.* New York:Wiley, 1989.

Reynolds, David K. Japanese Models of Psychotherapy. In Norbeck, E. and Lock, M., eds. *Health, Illness, and Medical Care in Japan.* Honolulu, University of Hawaii Press, 1987.

Reynolds, David K. Morita Psychotherapy. In Corsini, R., ed. *Handbook of Innovative Psychotherapies.* New York:Wiley, 1981.

Reynolds, David K. Naikan Therapy. In Corsini, R., ed. *Handbook of Innovative Psychotherapies.* New York:Wiley, 1981.

Reynolds, David K. Psychocultural Perspectives on Death. In Ahmed, P., ed. *Living and Dying with Cancer.* New York:Elsevier, 1981.

Reynolds, David K. Adaptations of Morita Therapy. *Japanese Journal of Psychotherapy,* 21 (1), 45-51, 1995.

Reynolds, David K. Psychodynamic insight and Morita psychotherapy. *Japanese Journal of Psychotherapy Research,* 5(4), 58-60, 1979.

Reynolds, David K. Naikan therapy--an experiential view. *International Journal of Social Psychiatry,* 23(4), 252-264, 1977.

Reynolds, David K. and Farberow, Norman L. *Suicide: Inside and Out.* Berkeley:University of California Press, 1976.

Reynolds, David K. and Farberow, Norman L. *Endangered Hope: Psychiatric Aftercare and Self Destruction.* Berkeley:University of California Press, 1977.

Reynolds, David K. and Farberow, Norman L. *The Family Shadow: Sources of Suicide and Schizophrenia.* Berkeley:University of California Press, 1981.

Reynolds, David K. and Farberow, Norman L. Suicide in Aftercare Facilities. In Parad, H. et al., *Emergency and Disaster Management.* New York:Charles Press, 1976.

Reynolds, David K. and Farberow, Norman L. The suicidal patient: An inside view. *Omega,* 4(3), 229-241, 1973. Abstracted in *Nursing Digest, Human Behavior,* and *1975 Review of Psychiatry.*

Reynolds, David K. and Farberow, Norman L. Experiential research: An inside perspective on suicide and social systems. *Life Threatening Behavior,* 3(4), 261-269. 1973. Abstracted in *Health Education Monographs,* 1975.

Reynolds, David K. and Kalish Richard A. The social ecology of dying:Observations of wards for the terminally ill. *Hospital and Community Psychiatry,* 25(3), 147-152, 1974.

Reynolds, David K. and Kalish, Richard A. Anticipation of futurity as a function of ethnicity and age. *Journal of Gerontology,* 29(2), 224-231, 1974.

Reynolds, David K., Kalish, Richard A., and Farberow, Norman L. A Cross Ethnic Study of Suicide Attitudes and Expectations in the United States. In Farberow, N.L., ed. *Suicide in Different Cultures.* Baltimore:University Park Press, 1975.

Reynolds, David K. and Kiefer, C.W. Cultural adaptability as an attribute of therapies: the case of Morita psychotherapy. *Culture, Medicine, and Psychiatry*, 1, 395-412, 1977.

Reynolds, David K. and Moacanin, Radmila. Eastern therapy: Western patient. *Japanese Journal of Psychotherapy Research*, 3, 305-316, 1976.

Reynolds, David K. and Yamamoto, Joe. East meets West: Moritist and Freudian psychotherapies. *Science and Psychoanalysis*, 21, 187-193, 1972. Abstracted in *Psychiatric Spectator*, 1972.

Reynolds, David K. and Nelson, Franklyn L. Personality, life situation and life expectancy. *Life Threatening Behavior,* 11(2), 99-110, 1981.

Reynolds, David K. and Yamamoto, Joe. Morita Psychotherapy in Japan. In Masserman, Jules, ed., *Current Psychiatric Therapies*, 13, 219-227, 1973.

Raush, Harold L. Transactions with therapists and the "real" world. Journal of Community Psycholog y, 7(2), 169-173, 1979.

Rokeach, Milton. The Three Christs of Ypsilanti: A Psychological Study. Knopf, New York, 1964.

Shibutani, Tamotsu. Reference groups as perspectives. Amer. J. Sociology 60(6), 562-569, 1955.

Shweder, Richard A. On savages and other children. American Anthropologist, 84(2), 354-366, 1982.

Spindler, George D., ed. Being an Anthropologist: Fieldwork in Eleven Cultures. Holt, 1970.

Strauss, Anselm. The Social Psychology of George Herbert Mead. University of Chicago Press, 1956.

Stryker, Sheldon (1959). Symbolic Interaction as an Approach to Family Research. Marriage and Family Living, May, 1959.

Szasa, Thomas S. The Manufacture of Madness. Harper and Row, 1970.

Troyer, William Lewis. Mead's social and functional theory of mind. Amer. Soc. Rev. 11(2), 1946, 198-202.

Wallace, Anthony F.C. and Raymond D. Fogelson. Biennial Review of Anthropology (2), 42-78, 1961.

Weitz, William A. Experiencing the role of a hospitalized psychiatric patient: A professional's view from the other side. Professional Psychology, 3(2), 1972, 151-154.